1000 days of Easy and Healthy Diabetic Diet Recipes for the Newly Diagnosed | 28-Day Meal Plan to Manage Type 2 Diabetes

TYPE 2 DIABETES COOKBOOK FOR BEGINNERS

Miranda Logan

© **Copyright 2022 All Right Reserved**

All rights reserved. No part of this guide may be reproduced in any form without permission in writing from the publisher except in the case of brief quotations embodied in critical articles or reviews.

Legal & Disclaimer

The information contained in this book and its contents is not designed to replace or take the place of any form of medical or professional advice; and is not meant to replace the need for independent medical, financial, legal or other professional advice or services, as may be required. The content and information in this book have been provided for educational and entertainment purposes only.

The content and information contained in this book has been compiled from sources deemed reliable, and it is accurate to the best of the Author's knowledge, information and belief. However, the Author cannot guarantee its accuracy and validity and cannot be held liable for any errors and/or omissions. Further, changes are periodically made to this book as and when needed. Where appropriate and/or necessary, you must consult a professional (including but not limited to your doctor, attorney, financial advisor or such other professional advisor) before using any of the suggested remedies, techniques, or information in this book.

Upon using the contents and information contained in this book, you agree to hold harmless the Author from and against any damages, costs, and expenses, including any legal fees potentially resulting from the application of any of the information provided by this book. This disclaimer applies to any loss, damages or injury caused by the use and application, whether directly or indirectly, of any advice or information presented, whether for breach of contract, tort, negligence, personal injury, criminal intent, or under any other cause of action.

You agree to accept all risks of using the information presented inside this book. You agree that by continuing to read this book, where appropriate and/or necessary, you shall consult a professional (including but not limited to your doctor, attorney, or financial advisor or such other advisor as needed) before using any of the suggested remedies, techniques, or information in this book.

About Author

My name is Miranda Logan I designs this cookbook. I am very passionate about cooking and an expert in designing the best recipes that are extremely healthy and proven useful for the masses. I got inspired to write this cookbook when I was diagnosed with type 2 diabetes. So, I found ways to control sugar levels and my weight through amazing recipes that worked well and helped me a lot in leading a normal life. I compiled all those recipes for the benefit of mankind, and here we go with this mind-blowing cookbook. In this cookbook, I put an extra effort into making sure that diabetic patients can get the most delicious recipes without increasing the glycaemic index of their bodies. The cookbook is designed with the utmost care and love that you will feel while following the best recipes for dealing with high carbohydrate levels.

I also take care of the calorie intake by the diabetic person per serving so that you will face no difficulty following these recipes, and you can control the glucose levels of your body quite easily. I include, the best food choices for people with diabetes, avoiding all the preserved food, high glucose items, fried items.

So, you will be carefree while preparing such recipes. I am proud to provide you with ultimate guidelines for preparing the best meal full of nutrition and hygiene.

I have worked very hard on this product, and I hope you like it!
Please, once you have finished reading it, could you support me with a review on Amazon?

Thank you!

★★★★★

CONTENTS

Before You Get Started 1
Why Insulin Is Not Forming? 1
Differences Between Type 1 And Type 2 Diabetes ... 2
Cause Of Type 2 Diabetes 3
Diet Trends 5
The Importance Of Exercise 6
Which Foods To Choose Or Avoid 6
Tips For Living Healthy With Diabetes 9
28-Day Meal Plan 10
Breakfast **16**
Cocoa-Chia Berry Pudding 17
Sweet Potato Hash Browns 17
Strawberry & Yogurt Parfait 18
Avocado Flaxseed Meal Smoothie 18
Shakshuka 19
Avocado Egg Tomato Waffle 19
Fluffy Banana Pancakes 20
Scramble Egg With Corn, Tomato, And Spinach ... 20
Brown Rice Pudding 21
Pineapple-Grapefruit Smoothie 21
Amaranth Porridge With Apples And Cinnamon ... 22
Broccoli And Cauliflower Sauté 22
Veggie Smoothie 23
Apple Muffins 23
Spinach Egg White Muffins 24
Tofu Scramble 24
Strawberry Power Parfait 25
French Toast With Berry Compote 25
Blueberry-Coconut Pudding 26
Mixed Fruit Cottage Cheese 26
Soups, Grain And Legumes **28**
Tomato Soup With Lentils 29
Chili Chicken Soup With Black Beans 29
Easy Tomato Soup 30
Asparagus Soup 30
Salmon Chowder Soup 31
Creamy Rich And Chicken Soup 31
Tofu And Seaweed Soup 32
Quinoa Brown Rice 32
Buckwheat Pancake With Buttermilk 33
Brown Rice With Mushroom 33
Barley Risotto With Zucchinis And Tomatoes ... 34
Rava Upma 34
Bean With Brown Rice 35
Black Bean Soup 35
Chicken And Black Bean Burritos 36
White Bean Chicken Chili 36

Red Lentils Stew 37
Baked Beans 37
Chickpea Stew With Spinach 38
Chickpea Curry With Sweet Potato 38
Spicy Black Chickpea Stew 39
Yellow Lentil Curry 39
Sweet And Creamy Corn 40
Corn Fritters 40
Snacks And Sandwiches **42**
Cinnamon Oatmeal Cookies With Raisins 43
Granola 43
Cucumber Sandwich 44
Energy Balls 44
Caprese Skewers 45
Carrot Energy Balls 45
Date & Pistachio Balls 46
Air-Fried Sweet Potato Chips 46
Zucchini Muffins 47
Dry Fruit Bits 47
Oat, Ginger, And Apricot Energy Balls 48
Air Fried Zucchini Chips 48
Veggie & Hummus Sandwich 49
Crispy Chickpeas 49
Pita Sandwich With Salmon 50
Strawberry & Cream Cheese Sandwich 50
Sauteed Fresh Corn With Herbs 51
Salads And Sides **52**
Spinach Smoothie 53
Perfect Cobb Salad 53
Shredded Carrot And Raisin Salad 54
Cheesy Casserole 54
Mushroom Gravy 55
Striped Cucumber Salad 55
Arugula Citrus Salad 56
Grilled Eggplant 56
Lemon Orzo 57
Carrot And Cucumber Salad 57
Creamy And Cheesy Chickpea Salad 58
Tomato, Onion & Cucumber Salad 58
Spinach, Walnuts & Strawberry Salad 59
Easy Cabbage Slaw 59
Spinach Avocado Smoothie 60
Grill Corn 60
Easy Potato Salad 61
Zucchini Pancakes 61
Sesame Green Beans 62
Corn And Black Bean Salad 62

Recipe	Page
Mango Chicken Salad	63
Roasted Brussels Sprouts With Pumpkin	63
Roasted Cauliflower Rice	64
Tuna & White Bean Salad	64
Corn Carrot Edamame Salad	65
Sautéed Garlic Green Beans	65
Easy Cucumber Kimchi	66
Bell Pepper Quinoa Salad	66
Kidney Beans And Brown Rice Salad	67
Air Fried Beets With Cottage Cheese	67
Lemon Broccoli Couscous	68
Spinach Blackberry Salad	68

Meat 70

Recipe	Page
Air-Fryer Beef Meatballs	71
Meat Sauce With Spaghetti	71
Grilled Veggie Beef Kebabs	72
Easy Meatloaf	72
Beef Casserole Stew	73
Stuffed Bell Peppers	73
Zucchini Boats	74
Sautéed Ground Beef And Beans	74
Beef Stir-Fry	75
Beef Stroganoff	75
Grill Beef Burgers	76
Air-Fryer Lamb Chops	76
Grilled Pork With Pineapple	77
Glazed Pork Chops	77
Grilled Beef Chimichangas	78
Beef Steak Fajitas	78
Pork Chops With Creamy Mushroom Sauce	79
Marinated Pork Skewer	79
Lamb And Veggies Stew	80
White Bean And Lamb Stew	80
Lamb Curry	81
Minced Lamb And Chickpeas	81
Broiled Lamb Chops	82
Baked Boneless Pork Chops In Tomato Sauce	82
Air Fryer Pork Dumplings	83
Pork Chop Casserole	83
Grilled Veggie Beef Kebabs	84

Poultry 86

Recipe	Page
Turkey Patties With Avocado Corn Salsa	87
Turkey Chili	87
Brown Rice With Chicken	88
Chicken Breast With Apple Sauce	88
Chicken Breast With Spanish And Cauliflower	89
Chicken Breast And Broccoli With Dill Sauce	89
Baked Chicken With Tomato Sauce	90
Dijon Baked Chicken	90
Chicken Thighs With Spinach	91
Chicken With Mushroom	91
Chicken Nuggets	92
Saucy Mediterranean Chicken	92
Creamy Chicken With White Sauce	93
Spinach And Cottage Stuffed Chicken	93
Chicken Broccoli Stir-Fry	94
Poached Chicken Breast	94
Shredded Chicken Chili	95
Prosciutto Wrapped Cream Cheese Chicken Breast	95
Oven-Baked Chicken Meatballs	96
Grilled Chicken Breast	96
Chicken & Chickpea Stew	97
Air Fried Chicken Thigh	97
Chicken Stew With Carrot	98
Chinese Chicken Curry	98
Chicken Curry	99

Fish And Seafood 100

Recipe	Page
Crumb Roasted Red Snapper	101
Red Pepper & Cottage Tilapia	101
Shrimp With Lemon Butter Sauce	102
Pistachio Crust Salomon	102
Lemony Parsley Baked Cod	103
Crab Cakes	103
Tuna Lettuce Wraps	104
Orange Tilapia In Parchment	104
Cajun Shrimp	105
Parmesan Baked Cod	105
Lemon-Pepper Tilapia	106
Cod With Stuffed Olives	106
Spiced Salmon	107
Spinach And Shrimp	107
Tomato Tuna Salad	108
Tilapia Fish Tacos	108
Cilantro Lime Shrimp	109
Cod With Bacon And Tomatoes	109
Pan Fried Shrimp And Mushrooms	110
Tequila Lime Shrimp Zoodles	110
Salmon And Veggies	111
Sweet Pepper Cod	111
Tuna Kabobs	112
Poached Salmon	112
Pan Fried Scallops	113
Chili Lime With Crunchy Shrimp	113
Cod With Pepper And Salsa	114
Seasoned Tilapia Fillets	114
Classic Grill Salmon	115
Salmon Stuffed Avocados	115

Desserts 116
- Brownies 117
- Cheesecake Bars 117
- Grill Pineapple 118
- Chocolate And Avocado Mousse 118
- Banana Sundae 119
- Vanilla Custard Berries 119
- Chocolate-Dipped Banana Bites 120
- Watermelon Pizza 120
- Peanut Butter Balls 121
- Strawberry, Chocolate, And Yogurt Bark 121
- Pineapple Sorbet 122
- Strawberry Sorbet 122
- Vegan Oatmeal Cookies 123
- Chocolate Chip Cookies 123
- Watermelon Sherbet 124
- Tofu Strawberry Smoothie 124
- Fresh Fruit Salad 125

Sauces, Dips And Dressings 126
- Tomato Sauce 127
- Cheese Sauce 127
- Tartar Sauce 128
- Alfredo Sauce 128
- Dill Dip 129
- Artichoke And Spinach Dip 129
- Yogurt Dip 130
- Black Bean Dip 130
- Ginger Carrot Dressing 131
- Onion Dip 131
- Citrus Salad Dressing 132
- Ranch Salad Dressing 132
- Blue Cheese Dressing 133
- Avocado Caesar Dressing 133
- Barbecue Sauce 134
- Food With Glycemic Index 135
- Measurement Conversion Chart 139
- Conclusion 140

BEFORE YOU GET STARTED

Diabetes is an alarming disease that is prevailing much faster nowadays. People are much concerned to protect their bodies from infections and diseases and this requires knowledge and up-to-date information on modes of transfer of the disease, its cure, prevention and treatment. So, talking about diabetes is a disease which is characterized by increased blood sugar levels or Hyperglycaemia. The body requires energy from the food we eat. The carbohydrates present in the food are broken down into simpler substances or monosaccharides such as glucose. From blood, the glucose is passed onto body cells where it is broken down by glycolysis to provide energy.

In diabetic patients, the glucose is not transferred to cells and hence the quantity of glucose gets increased in the blood causing hyperglycaemia. You must be wondering why this glucose is not going to the cells? Well, there is a big reason for it. It is due to the deficiency of a hormone called insulin which is released from the beta cells of the pancreas. The pancreas is a vital endocrine organ present in the abdominal region behind and below the stomach. It has two major types of cells. The alpha cells release the glucagon hormone and the beta cells which release insulin.

WHY INSULIN IS NOT FORMING?

- **THE PANCREAS IS NOT PRODUCING INSULIN DUE TO DAMAGE TO BETA CELLS.**
- **THE PANCREAS IS PRODUCING INSULIN BUT IT IS NOT ENOUGH FOR THE BODY'S USE.**
- **THE PANCREAS IS PRODUCING SUFFICIENT INSULIN BUT CELLS ARE NOT INCORPORATING IT. THEY ARE MISSING THOSE RECEPTORS THAT ALLOW INSULIN TO ENTER THE CELLS.**

DEPENDING UPON THE REASONS FOR THE ONSET OF DIABETES, WE CAN BROADLY CLASSIFY INSULIN INTO FOUR MAJOR TYPES:

- **DIABETES TYPE 1**
- **DIABETES TYPE 2**
- **PREDIABETES**
- **GESTATIONAL DIABETES**

THESE TYPES DIFFER IN A LOT OF WAYS. IN THE FOLLOWING SECTION, YOU WILL GET TO KNOW THE DIFFERENCES BETWEEN TYPE 1 DIABETES AND TYPE 2 DIABETES.

DIFFERENCES BETWEEN TYPE 1 AND TYPE 2 DIABETES

Before starting differences, you must know what is meant by type 1 and type 2.

Type 1 Diabetes:

Type 1 refers to diabetes in which beta cells of the pancreas are destroyed due to any autoimmune disease. The insulin is not produced sufficiently because around 90% of beta cells that produce insulin are lost. Hence, the body is dependent on external insulin sources so it is called insulin-dependent diabetes. On average 5% to 10% of diabetic patients have this type 1 disease.

Genetic and environmental factors can also be a reason to type 1 diabetes. If your parents or siblings have this disease, you are more likely to be prone to this disease. Also, any viral infection or nutritional deficiency can cause the immune system to destroy the beta cells that are responsible for making insulin. Hence, no insulin leads to the accumulation of glucose or sugar in the blood causing hyperglycaemia which is called diabetes.

Diabetes type 1 starts in early childhood or adult age. Hence, also called juvenile-onset diabetes.

Type 2 Diabetes:

Type 2 diabetes is more frequent in the world. About 90% of diabetic patients are suffering from type 2 diabetes. It affects more of the obese population of the world. People who have a lethargic lifestyle and are overweight are more prone to type 2 diabetes.

The pathophysiology of type 2 diabetes is that the body is insulin resistant. Either the pancreas is not producing enough insulin, or the body is not responding to the insulin present in the blood. The result is excessive glucose levels in the blood, and the body cells, such as liver cells and muscle cells are deprived of glucose and hence the energy. So, giving insulin can't solve the issue because the body is not picking it up. So, type 2 diabetes is also called insulin-independent diabetes. Many factors can contribute to type 2 diabetes such as obesity. People who are obese are most likely to get diabetes type 2. Studies show that 80% to 90% of obese get type 2 diabetes. There is no possible cure for diabetes, only lifestyle modifications can help to alleviate the symptoms. Losing weight is a good step to control diabetes. Also, developing daily habits of doing exercise is very beneficial for diabetic patients. Doing exercise 4 days per week is advisable. The duration of exercise must be half an hour daily.

Effects Of Diabetes:

Diabetes affects almost every organ of the body. The major organs affected are the eyes, kidneys, and brain. The diabetic will suffer from the following issues:

Retinopathy:
Due to increased glucose levels in the body, the eyes will suffer from cataracts and glaucoma.

Neuropathy:
Nerves are affected due to hyperglycaemic condition and there is numbness and decreased sensation in the lower limb.

Nephropathy:
The nephron is the functional unit of the kidneys. Diabetes affects all the areas of tubules in the kidneys and there is increased glucose level in the urine. All these conditions will lead to chronic kidney disease.

CAUSE OF TYPE 2 DIABETES

There are many causes of type 2 diabetes, the most common are listed below:

Obesity:

Obesity is the number one cause of diabetes type 2. Almost 90% of diabetic patients are obese. People who are obese have less tendency to perform physical activities and have an accumulation of unhealthy fats inside the body. The vital organs such as the liver, kidneys and heart are affected by unhealthy cholesterol levels in the body. According to research, non-alcoholic fatty liver disease is triggered by diabetes.

Non-alcoholic fatty liver disease can lead to cirrhosis and ultimately liver carcinomas. These conditions are fatal for the body because the liver is involved in many vital functions of the body. The liver acts as a storehouse of glycogen and in fasting time, through the process of glycogenolysis, the glycogen is converted to glucose. Glucose is the prime molecule for energy and acts as the only source of energy for the brain and RBCs. Brain and RBCs only rely on glucose for energy, but when the body is not having enough glucose, then tissue death in the brain can occur which ultimately causes death.

Physical inactivity:

People who have a sluggish lifestyle are also more likely to suffer from diabetes type 2. It is recommended that a person must have a daily exercise routine of at least half an hour or 150 minutes per week. Exercise is the best thing we can do for our bodies. People who do exercise daily are most likely to prevent harmful diseases. They are more active, agile and vigilant in their duties and jobs. In the following, the benefits of exercise are listed that can help you to know the importance of exercise.

Genetic history:

Genes and family history are also main factors if you are diagnosed with type 2 diabetes. If your parents or siblings have type 2, you are most likely to suffer from it but keeping a healthy lifestyle can help you to prevent it.

Geographical background:

People who belong to Hispania, Alaska, Africa and South America are more likely to get type 2 diabetes. The reason might be the gene pool or the lifestyle of those regions.

Dysfunction of pancreatic cells:

As the pancreas are responsible for the production of vital hormones such as insulin and glucagon, so if there is any dysfunction in pancreatic cells, then it is directly related with onset of diabetes. Thus, it is extremely important to keep in check the proper functioning of pancreatic cells.

Insulin resistance:

Insulin resistance is a condition when the body is producing insulin but the cells of the body are resisting its function. Either the insulin receptors which are referred to as GLUT are not taking insulin, so the glucose is not entering the body and hence energy levels are low. The cell may die when they don't get energy. There are some cells such as the red blood cells and those present in the brain which are reliant on glucose for energy. In case of insufficient energy from glycolysis, tissue death may start.

How to Prevent and Control It

Talking about the prevention of diabetes, it is essential to know the symptoms and have the basic knowledge of this disease. Keep in mind that there is no possible cure for this disease. If you get it, then there are just lifestyle modifications that can help you in avoiding the severity of the issue. The patients with diabetes mostly present with the following symptoms:

Symptoms of diabetes:

Polyuria:
The diabetic person will complain of frequent urination all the time. polyuria refers to an increased volume of urine.

Polydipsia:
The person will have increased thirst. As the body is losing a great amount of water through urine, so to balance the fluid content, the person will tend to drink more and more water. The increased thirst is a very important symptom of diabetes.

Increased hunger:
The cells of the body are not getting glucose which is the prime energy source of the body, hence the body is in constant demand of energy. So, the person will always feel hungry despite that he is continuously eating which is, in turn, unhealthy for the body.

Prevention:

It is well said that "Prevention is better than cure". Diabetes can affect your entire body, so if you want to prevent this disease you can follow the below mentioned preventive measures:

Eat less refined sugars:
In all the bakery items, and fast foods you will get refined sugars. Refined sugars break down easily and they provide an instant source of energy increasing blood sugar levels. So, you must decrease the intake of refined carbohydrates. Instead, complex carbohydrates are good for your body. Nowadays, eating brown sugar and brown rice is advisable by experts, the reason is that they take a longer time for breakdown and hence provide energy for a longer time. the fibre content also provides a feeling of fullness and hence a person will eat less.

Losing weight:
Losing some extra weight can also help you to prevent diabetes. Experts say that losing 7% of your body weight, for example, if you have 70 kg mass, then losing 5 to 7 kg can help you to avoid diabetes. The harmful fat content will also get lost and you can have a fit and active body.

Exercise:
As mentioned earlier, the daily routine of exercise is the best thing for your body. You have to spare some time for your body. Doing exercise for just 15 minutes a day can help you to eliminate the chances of infections and diseases. So, make it a firm habit to do exercise daily. Exercise can also help you to be active all day long, so you can have the best chance to perform your work well. being sluggish and lazy will affect your entire day schedule, so to avoid that you have to invest your time in workouts and exercise daily.

Control of diabetes:

If the person gets diabetes, then the next step is to lower the glucose levels in the blood. There are multiple strategies in this regard.

Type 1 diabetes:

In type 1, the doctor can advise using insulin injections before meals. As the body is not preparing insulin for type 1, so when you give the artificial insulin, it can help the body to shunt glucose inside the cells and hence the body can get energy from various glycolytic pathways.

Also, developing a healthy lifestyle, like exercise, a balanced diet and avoiding unhealthy carbohydrates and fats is the ultimate cure for your condition.

Type 2 diabetes:

As type 2 is non-insulin-dependent because the issue is insulin resistance rather than the production of insulin, getting an external source of insulin might not help. In type 2, the only control is lifestyle modifications. Getting a balanced and healthy diet containing fresh vegetables and more fibre content is best for your body. Also, exercise can make a difference because you will lose your extra weight and also insulin resistant cells might start functioning because of the healthy effect of exercise on your body.

Drugs:

There is no one-stop drug that a diabetic person can get and he is free from disease. It is incurable but you can lessen the severity of the disease by getting a healthy diet, losing fats and doing exercise daily. However, some drugs like Metformin are believed to have some beneficial role in curing diabetes.

DIET TRENDS

Many diets are advised by experts that can have very good effects on diabetic conditions. In the following section, you can have an overview of top diets that are helpful:

Keto diet:

In the keto diet, the carbohydrate content is reduced to 50 grams per day which is minimal. The body starts relying on ketone sources and fats. You can lose weight by following this diet. Also, it improves the metabolic conditions of the body.

Atkins diet:

In the Atkins diet, there is very low carbohydrate intake but you can change the amount slightly and hence you can't get bored by following one diet routine for a long time. it is also very good for getting the best metabolism.

Intermittent fasting:

In this type of diet, a person takes a meal but after that takes a break from all kinds of food for like 8 to 10 hours. You just have to drink water during your "fast". This diet will help the body to have the maximum time to digest and absorb the meal. Hence, the body can't make reserves of fats which are unhealthy for the body. Very good for people who are planning to have the best diet schedule.

Paleo diet:

Paleo eliminated the grain content. It is also good for those who are planning to have a low carb diet and hence get a healthy body and a healthy mind!

THE IMPORTANCE OF EXERCISE

- DAILY EXERCISE CAN HELP A PERSON TO STAY CALM AND HAPPY.
- PERFORMING EXERCISE DAILY HELPS TO INCREASE BLOOD FLOW TO EVERY CELL OF THE BODY.
- EXERCISE IS BEST FOR GLOWING SKIN.
- SWEATING WHILE EXERCISING IS AN INDICATION OF BURNING FAT RESERVES.
- YOU CAN LOSE WEIGHT MUCH FASTER BY HAVING STRENUOUS EXERCISE.
- EXERCISE CAN ALSO HELP A PERSON STRENGTHEN BONES AND JOINTS. IT IS GOOD FOR THE MUSCULAR SYSTEM AS WELL.
- PEOPLE WITH FIRM HABITS OF EXERCISE CAN PREVENT CHRONIC DISEASES OF ALL KINDS.
- EXERCISE HAS A POSITIVE EFFECT ON MEMORY AND THE BRAIN AS WELL. SO, STARTING YOUR DAY WITH 15 MINUTES OF EXERCISE OR HALF AN HOUR OF BRISK WALKING CAN HELP YOU TO PERFORM WELL IN YOUR STUDIES AND COLLEGE.

WHICH FOODS TO CHOOSE OR AVOID

The diet plays a key role in making the condition better or worse for a diabetic patient. A diabetic must follow a proper diet chart that is designed keeping in view the condition of the patient. Even the prediabetic patients (those who are not having diabetes but are most likely to have it in future) must follow a healthy diet routine.

SEEDS AND NUTS

SEEDS AND NUTS TO CHOOSE	SEEDS AND NUTS TO AVOID
- Flaxseeds/linseeds - Almonds and peanuts - Cashew nuts and chia seeds - Pistachios and macadamia - Pumpkin seeds and fennel seeds	- Sweet sugar coated corn - Chocolate covered peanuts - Sugar coated cashews and chia - Honey coated nuts - Raisins

FATS AND OILS

FATS AND OILS TO CHOOSE	FATS AND OILS TO AVOID
- Salmon and tuna oil - Canola oil and sunflower oil - Olive oil - Flaxseed oil - Mono Unsaturated and polyunsaturated fats	- Butter - Palm oil - Coconut oil - Omega 6 fatty acids - Saturated fats

SWEETS

SWEETS TO CHOOSE	SWEETS TO AVOID
- Artificial sweeteners such as aspartame - Stevia - Sorbitol - Dark chocolate	- Jams and jellies - Desserts - Candy and chocolates - Baked cookies

VEGETABLES

VEGETABLES TO CHOOSE	VEGETABLES TO AVOID
- Fresh vegetables - Plain frozen vegetables - Low sodium canned vegetables	- Canned vegetables with high sodium - Vegetables with butter or cheese - Pickles

LEGUMES

LEGUMES TO CHOOSE	LEGUMES TO AVOID
- Lentils - Black beans and red kidney beans - Lima and pinto beans - Dried peas	- Raw lentils - White kidney beans - Broad beans - Castor beans

WHOLE GRAINS

WHOLE GRAINS TO CHOOSE	WHOLE GRAINS TO AVOID
- Brown rice - Oatmeal - Quinoa - Millet and amaranth	- White rice - White flour - White bread - White Pasta

PROTEINS

PROTEINS TO CHOOSE	PROTEINS TO AVOID
- Egg whites - Plant based Beans, nuts and seeds - White meat - Fish, turkey and sea food - Meat cooked in less fats and oil	- Salami and ham - Sausages - Deep fried fish and sea food - Fried chicken - Pork bacon

DAIRY ITEMS

DAIRY ITEMS TO CHOOSE	DAIRY ITEMS TO AVOID
- Low fat cottage cheese - Non-fat plain yogurt - Unsweetened almond and soy milk - Skimmed milk	- Full fat or sweetened yogurt - Full fat cheese - Flavoured and sweetened milk - Full fat sweetened kefir

TIPS FOR LIVING HEALTHY WITH DIABETES

1. **AVOID CARBOHYDRATE-RICH FOOD AS THE BODY IS ALREADY DEALING WITH HIGH GLUCOSE LEVELS IN THE BLOOD.**

2. **DO EXERCISE DAILY AS IT PROVIDES MULTIPLE BENEFITS. IT CAN MAKE YOU MORE FIT, HEALTHY AND ACTIVE.**

3. **DO YOGA DAILY. YOGA IS THE BEST THERAPY EXERCISE FOR DIABETICS. IT ALSO HELPS TO LOSE UNHEALTHY WEIGHT**

4. **LOSE WEIGHT IF YOU ARE OBESE. OBESITY CAN CAUSE DIABETES, SO KEEP YOUR WEIGHT UNDER CONTROL.**

5. **DRINK BLACK COFFEE.**

6. **AVOID STRESSFUL CONDITIONS. STRESS CAN CAUSE HYPERTENSION AND HIGH BLOOD PRESSURE. IT ALSO WORSENS THE CONDITION OF DIABETICS.**

7. **KEEP YOUR BLOOD SUGAR LEVELS RECORDED ON DAILY BASIS.**

8. **KEEP IN CONTACT WITH YOUR DOCTOR.**

28-DAY MEAL PLAN

1ST WEEK MEAL PLAN

MONDAY
BREAKFAST	LUNCH	DINNER	SNACKS
Strawberry & Yogurt Parfait P#18	Tuna & White Bean Salad P#64	Chickpea Curry with Sweet Potato P#38	Energy Balls P#44

TUESDAY
BREAKFAST	LUNCH	DINNER	SNACKS
Cocoa-Chia Berry Pudding P#17	Meat Sauce with Spaghetti P#71	Brown rice with chicken P#88	Granola P#43

WEDNESDAY
BREAKFAST	LUNCH	DINNER	SNACKS
Shakshuka P#19	Crab Cakes P#103	Zucchini Boats P#74	Cheesecake Bars P#117

THURSDAY
BREAKFAST	LUNCH	DINNER	SNACKS
Scramble Egg with Corn, Tomato, and Spinach P#20	Salmon Stuffed Avocados P#115	Red Lentils Stew P#37	Zucchini Muffins P#47

FRIDAY
BREAKFAST	LUNCH	DINNER	SNACKS
Amaranth Porridge with Apples and Cinnamon P#22	Chicken & Chickpea Stew P#97	Salmon and Veggies P#111	Chocolate and Avocado Mousse P#118

SATURDAY
BREAKFAST	LUNCH	DINNER	SNACKS
Brown Rice Pudding P#21	Pistachio Crust Salomon P#102	Beef Steak Fajitas P#78	Air Fried Zucchini Chips P#48

SUNDAY
BREAKFAST	LUNCH	DINNER	SNACKS
Tofu Scramble P#24	Perfect Cobb Salad P#53	Easy Meatloaf P#72	Vegan Oatmeal Cookies P#123

Diabetes Cookbook

2ND WEEK MEAL PLAN

MONDAY
BREAKFAST	LUNCH	DINNER	SNACKS
Cocoa-Chia Berry Pudding P#17	Chili Chicken Soup with Black Beans P#29	Brown rice with chicken P#88	Chocolate and Avocado Mousse P#118

TUESDAY
BREAKFAST	LUNCH	DINNER	SNACKS
Blueberry-Coconut pudding P#26	Perfect Cobb Salad P#53	Tilapia Fish Tacos P#108	Air Fried Zucchini Chips P#48

WEDNESDAY
BREAKFAST	LUNCH	DINNER	SNACKS
Mixed Fruit Cottage Cheese P#26	Salmon Stuffed Avocados P#115	Salmon Chowder Soup P#31	Carrot Energy Balls P#45

THURSDAY
BREAKFAST	LUNCH	DINNER	SNACKS
Amaranth Porridge with Apples and Cinnamon P#22	Yellow Lentil Curry P#39	Marinated Pork Skewer P#79	Dry Fruit Bits P#47

FRIDAY
BREAKFAST	LUNCH	DINNER	SNACKS
Chocolate Chip Cookies P#20	Cheesy Casserole P#54	Poached Salmon P#112	Veggie & Hummus Sandwich P#49

SATURDAY
BREAKFAST	LUNCH	DINNER	SNACKS
Brown Rice Pudding P#21	Crumb Roasted Red Snapper P#101	Chicken Breast and Broccoli with Dill Sauce P#89	Chocolate Chip Cookies P#123

SUNDAY
BREAKFAST	LUNCH	DINNER	SNACKS
Tofu Scramble P#24	Creamy Rich and Chicken Soup P#31	Beef Steak Fajitas P#78	Zucchini Muffins P#47

Diabetes Cookbook

3RD WEEK MEAL PLAN

MONDAY
BREAKFAST	LUNCH	DINNER	SNACKS
Avocado Flaxseed meal Smoothie P#18	Kidney Beans and Brown Rice Salad P#67	Brown rice with chicken P#88	Air Fried Zucchini Chips P#48

TUESDAY
BREAKFAST	LUNCH	DINNER	SNACKS
Avocado Egg Tomato Waffle P#19	Rava Upma P#34	Air Fried Chicken Thigh P#97	Chocolate and Avocado Mousse P#118

WEDNESDAY
BREAKFAST	LUNCH	DINNER	SNACKS
Scramble Egg with Corn, Tomato, and Spinach P#20	Tilapia Fish Tacos P#108	Chinese Chicken Curry P#98	Chocolate Chip Cookies P#123

THURSDAY
BREAKFAST	LUNCH	DINNER	SNACKS
Blueberry-Coconut pudding P#26	Chicken Nuggets P#91	Pork Chop Casserole P#83	Zucchini Muffins P#47

FRIDAY
BREAKFAST	LUNCH	DINNER	SNACKS
Strawberry Power Parfait P#25	Chickpea Stew with Spinach P#38	Barley Risotto with Zucchinis and Tomatoes P#38	Cheesecake Bars P#117

SATURDAY
BREAKFAST	LUNCH	DINNER	SNACKS
Chicken and Black Bean Burritos P#36	Meat Sauce with Spaghetti P#71	Pork Chops with Creamy Mushroom Sauce P#79	Air Fried Zucchini Chips P#48

SUNDAY
BREAKFAST	LUNCH	DINNER	SNACKS
Mixed Fruit Cottage Cheese P#26	Salmon Chowder Soup P#31	Salmon and Veggies P#111	Tofu Strawberry Smoothie P#124

Diabetes Cookbook

4TH WEEK MEAL PLAN

MONDAY

BREAKFAST	LUNCH	DINNER	SNACKS
Strawberry & Yogurt Parfait P#18	Tuna & White Bean Salad P#64	Crumb Roasted Red Snapper P#101	Zucchini Muffins P#47

TUESDAY

BREAKFAST	LUNCH	DINNER	SNACKS
Cocoa-Chia Berry Pudding P#17	Sautéed Ground Beef and Beans P#74	Chili Lime with Crunchy Shrimp P#113	Air Fried Zucchini Chips P#48

WEDNESDAY

BREAKFAST	LUNCH	DINNER	SNACKS
Fluffy Banana Pancakes P#20	Roasted Brussels Sprouts with Pumpkin P#63	Tuna Lettuce Wraps P#104	Chocolate and Avocado Mousse P#118

THURSDAY

BREAKFAST	LUNCH	DINNER	SNACKS
Shakshuka P#19	Creamy Rich and Chicken Soup P#31	Glazed Pork Chops P#77	Cheesecake Bars P#117

FRIDAY

BREAKFAST	LUNCH	DINNER	SNACKS
Buckwheat Pancake with Buttermilk P#33	Chicken & Chickpea Stew P#97	Spicy Black Chickpea Stew P#39	Vanilla Custard Berries P#119

SATURDAY

BREAKFAST	LUNCH	DINNER	SNACKS
Avocado Egg Tomato Waffle P#19	Barley Risotto with Zucchinis and Tomatoes P#34	White bean and lamb stew P#80	Chocolate Chip Cookies P#123

SUNDAY

BREAKFAST	LUNCH	DINNER	SNACKS
Avocado Flaxseed meal Smoothie P#18	Brown rice with chicken P#88	Tequila Lime Shrimp Zoodles P#110	Tofu Strawberry Smoothie P#124

Diabetes Cookbook

BREAKFAST

SWEET POTATO HASH BROWNS

Nutritional Info: Calories: 103cal, Total fat: 24g, Saturated fat: 11.5g, Protein: 4.8g, Carbs: 42.3g, Sodium: 301mg, Fiber: 3.1g, Sugar: 6g

Ingredients

- 1½ cups peeled and grated sweet potato
- ½ tbsp. extra-virgin olive oil, divided
- 1 tsp. minced garlic
- ½ tbsp. chopped shallot
- Salt and ground pepper as per taste

Instructions

1. Add shredded sweet potato, shallot, garlic, ½ tsp oil, salt, and pepper in a large bowl. Add ½ tsp oil and put it in a large cast-iron skillet over medium-high heat. Using a spatula, flatten three 1/2-cup patties in the pan.
2. Cook the sweet potato patties until browned on both sides, 6 to 8 minutes total, turning once, and decrease the stove heat to medium if the pan becomes too hot.
3. Cover and place on a baking sheet to keep warm. Continue with the leftover ½ tbsp oil and sweet potato mixture.

Preparing time 10, Total time 20, Servings 1, Serving size 1 patty

COCOA-CHIA BERRY PUDDING

Nutritional Info: Calories: 222cal, Total fat: 11g, Saturated fat: 1g, Protein: 6g, Carbs: 27.5g, Sodium: 91mg, Fiber: 12.8g, Sugar: 11.2g

Ingredients

- ½ cup unsweetened almond milk
- 2 tbsp. chia seeds
- ½ tsp. unsweetened cocoa powder
- ¼ tsp. vanilla extract
- ½ cup fresh mixed berries, divided

Instructions

1. Add almond milk, chia, syrup, cocoa, and vanilla to a small serving bowl. Cover; leave in refrigerate for at least 8 hours.
2. Stir well when ready to serve. Add pudding into a serving glass or bowl, then place berries on top. Stir, serve and enjoy.

Preparing time 8 hours, Total time 8 hours 10 minutes, Servings 1, Serving size 1 cup

STRAWBERRY & YOGURT PARFAIT

Nutritional Info: Calories: 285cal, Total fat: 8g, Saturated fat: 1g, Protein: 17g, Carbs: 37g, Sodium: 49.8mg, Fiber: 6g, Sugar: 14g

Ingredients

- 1 cup sliced fresh strawberries
- 1 tsp. stevia
- ½ cup nonfat yogurt
- 4 tbsp. granola

Instructions

1. Add some sliced strawberries to the glass base, place a layer of yogurt, drizzle stevia, and add a layer of granola.
2. Top with remaining sliced strawberries. Stir, serve, and enjoy.

Preparing time 10 minutes, Total time 10 minutes, Servings: 1, Serving size 1-1/2 cups

AVOCADO FLAXSEED MEAL SMOOTHIE

Nutritional Info: Calories: 595cal, Total fat: 18g, Saturated fat: 2g, Protein: 4.3g, Carbs: 33g, Sodium: 8mg, Fiber: 9g, Sugar: 13g

Ingredients

- 1¼ cups unsweetened almond milk
- ½ small avocado, peeled and sliced
- 1 small banana, sliced
- ¼ cup ice
- 1 tbsp flaxseed

Instructions

1. Add all elements to the high-power blender and blend them well until they turn in a smooth form.
2. Pour the mixture into the glass. Serve and enjoy.

Preparing time 10 minutes, Total time 10 minutes, Servings: 1, Serving size 1 serving jar

Diabetes Cookbook

AVOCADO EGG TOMATO WAFFLE

Nutritional Info: Calories: 209cal, Total fat: 12g, Saturated fat: 2g, Protein: 9g, Carbs: 17g, Sodium: 279mg, Fiber: 6g, Sugar: 2g

Ingredients

- 1 frozen whole-grain waffle
- 1 egg
- ½ tbsp. olive oil
- ½ of a small avocado, peeled and sliced
- 1 tbsp. fresh salsa or chopped tomato
- Salt and pepper to taste

Instructions

1. Add ½ tbsp oil to the pan, put it over medium heat, add the egg, and cook as you like. Toast the waffle as per the steps on the package. Place avocado slices, a fried egg, and a waffle on a plate.
2. Top with chopped tomato or tomato salsa and season with salt and pepper to taste. Serve and have fun.

Preparing time 10 minutes, Total time 10 minutes, Servings: 1,
Serving size 1 waffle, fried egg, 1/2 sliced avocado

SHAKSHUKA

Nutritional Info: Calories: 235cal, Total fat: 16.5g, Saturated fat: 4g, Protein: 14g, Carbs: 8g, Sodium: 390mg, Fiber: 2g, Sugar: 3g

Ingredients

- ½ tbsp. extra virgin olive oil
- ¼ cup chopped onion
- 1 tsp. minced garlic
- ¼ tsp. cumin powder
- Salt and pepper
- 100g tomatoes, halved
- 2 large eggs
- ¼ cup chopped baby spinach

Instructions

1. Preheat the oven to 400. Take a large skillet, add oil, and put it over medium. Add onion and cook for 8 minutes, or until golden brown and tender. Now add garlic, cumin, salt, and pepper. Stir in the tomatoes, then roast for 10 minutes in the oven.
2. Remove the pan, stir well, then make 2 small wells in the vegetable mixture, carefully cracking one egg. Bake eggs until done to your liking, about 7 to 8 minutes, for slightly runny yolks. Serve with toast, if desired, and a sprinkle of spinach.

Preparing time 10 minutes, Total time 35 minutes, Servings: 1,
Serving size 1 serving plate (about 8 oz)

Diabetes Cookbook

FLUFFY BANANA PANCAKES

Nutritional Info: Calories: 124cal, Total fat: 4g, Saturated fat: 1g, Protein: 7g, Carbs: 14g, Sodium: 72mg, Fiber: 1.5g, Sugar: 7g

Ingredients

- 1 large egg
- 1 small ripe banana

Instructions

1. In a high-power blender, puree the eggs and banana until smooth. Take a large nonstick skillet, add oil, and put it over medium heat. Pour one portion of the batter into the pan after dividing the batter into three portions.
2. Cook for 2-4 mins, or until bubbles appear on the surface and the edges dry. Flip the pancakes gently with a thin spatula and cook for 1 to 2 minutes more, or until browned on the bottom.
3. Place the pancakes on a plate and set them aside. Repeat with the remaining batter, re-oiling the pan if necessary.

Preparing time 5 minutes, Total time 10 minutes, Servings 1

SCRAMBLE EGG WITH CORN, TOMATO, AND SPINACH

Nutritional Info: Calories: 296cal, Total fat: 19g, Saturated fat: 4g, Protein: 18g, Carbs: 21g, Sodium: 394mg, Fiber: 7g, Sugar: 5g

Ingredients

- 1 tsp. olive oil
- 1½ fresh cups baby spinach
- 2 large eggs, lightly beaten
- Salt and ground pepper
- 2 cherry tomatoes, quartered
- 2 tbsp. canned corn
- 1 slice of whole-grain bread, toasted

Instructions

1. Take a small nonstick skillet, add oil, and put it over medium-high heat. Break the eggs one by one and add them to the skillet. Cook, stirring until scramble, to ensure even cooking, for 1 to 2 minutes, or until just set.
2. Add salt and pepper to taste. Serve the scrambled egg with toast bread, tomatoes, and corn. Serve and enjoy.

Preparing time 5 minutes, Total time 10 minutes, Servings 1

Diabetes Cookbook

PINEAPPLE-GRAPEFRUIT SMOOTHIE

Nutritional Info: Calories: 108cal, Total fat: 2g, Saturated fat: 0.25g, Protein: 3g, Carbs: 21g, Sodium: 5mg, Fiber: 3g, Sugar: 4g

Ingredients

- ¼ cup fresh coconut water
- ¼ cup fresh diced pineapple
- ½ cup fresh baby spinach
- ¼ cup fresh grapefruit juice
- ½ tsp. grated fresh ginger
- 1 cup ice

Instructions

1. Combine coconut water, pineapple, baby spinach, grapefruit, ginger, and ice in a high-powered blender in a high-powered blender.
2. Puree until all the elements turn in a smooth and frothy form. Serve and enjoy.

Preparing time 5 minutes, Total time 10 minutes, Servings: 1

BROWN RICE PUDDING

Nutritional Info: Calories: 272cal, Total fat: 8g, Saturated fat: 2g, Protein: 6g, Carbs: 47g, Sodium: 281mg, Fiber: 6g, Sugar: 10g

Ingredients

- 2 tbsp. brown rice
- ¾ cup unsweetened almond milk
- 1 tsp. olive oil
- 3-4 drops of pure vanilla extract
- 2 tbsp. raisins
- ½ tbsp. chia seeds
- ¼ cup chopped cherries and blueberries
- 1 tbsp. unsweetened cherry sauce
- 1 tbsp. nonfat yogurt

Instructions

1. Rinse rice completely in cold running water until the water is clear; drain. Combine rice, ½ cup milk, oil, and vanilla extract in a medium pot. Cover the pot and boil. Then decrease the stove heat to low and cook for 20 minutes.
2. Remove from the heat and stir in the rest of the milk, raisins, and chia seeds. Allow 5 minutes for the pudding to set after stirring. Pour cherry sauce, berries, and yogurt into a serving bowl and gently stir to combine. Serve and enjoy.

Preparing time 5 minutes, Total time 30 minutes, Servings: 1

AMARANTH PORRIDGE WITH APPLES AND CINNAMON

Nutritional Info: Calories: 360cal, Total fat: 12g, Saturated fat: 6.5g, Protein: 10g, Carbs: 54g, Sodium: 84mg, Fiber: 6g, Sugar: 12g

Ingredients

- 4 tbsp. amaranth
- ¾ cup soy milk
- ½ tsp. cinnamon
- 1 tsp. vanilla extract
- 1 tbsp. coconut oil
- 1 small apple, chopped

Instructions

1. Take a small saucepan, and add amaranth, milk, cinnamon, and vanilla. Put the pan over medium-high heat; take a boil, then simmer for 15 minutes.
2. Then remove from heat; cover it for another 5 minutes to thicken. In a skillet, add coconut oil, and put it over low heat. Toss in the apples with the last of the cinnamon. Stir in the apples and cook for 5 minutes, or until they soften.
3. In a bowl, combine the amaranth and apples. If desired, add more coconut milk to the mix. Warm the dish before serving.

Preparing time 5 minutes, Total time 30 minutes, Servings 1

BROCCOLI AND CAULIFLOWER SAUTÉ

Nutritional Info: Calories: 47cal, Total fat: 2.4g, Saturated fat: 0.5g, Protein: 1.5g, Carbs: 4g, Sodium: 88mg, Fiber: 1.3g, Sugar: 1g

Ingredients

- ¼ cup cauliflower florets
- ½ tsp. olive oil
- ¼ cup broccoli florets
- 1 tsp. minced garlic
- 1 tbsp. low-sodium chicken broth
- 1 tbsp. water
- Salt and ground black pepper

Instructions

1. Add oil to the large skillet and put it over medium-high heat until shimmering. Place in broccoli, cauliflower, and garlic, and cook for 2 mins until tender. Reduce the stove heat to low and carefully add the broth, water, salt, pepper, cover, and cook for 2 minutes.
2. Then uncover and turn the stove heat to medium. Cook for 2 minutes until the vegetables are tender, stirring occasionally.

Preparing time 5 minutes, Total time 12 minutes, Servings 1

Diabetes Cookbook

APPLE MUFFINS

Nutritional Info: Calories: 98cal, Total fat: 2.5g, Saturated fat: 0.6g, Protein: 3g, Carbs: 17g, Sodium: 215mg, Fiber: 0.8g, Sugar: 1.9g

Ingredients

- 2 ½ tsp. baking powder
- vegetable oil
- 1 tbsp. low-fat milk
- 1 small egg, lightly beaten
- 1 tsp monk fruit sweetener
- 1½ tsp. low-fat margarine, melted
- 1 tbsp. minced apple
- 2 tbsp. all-purpose flour
- Pinch ground cinnamon
- Salt to taste
- Pinch of nutmeg powder

Instructions

1. Preheat the oven range to 400 degrees F (200 degrees C). Prepare 2 muffin cups with cooking spray.
2. Mix flour, baking powder, sweetener, cinnamon, sea salt, and nutmeg in a large bowl. Beat milk, egg, and margarine in a separate bowl; add to flour mixture and stir just till the dry mix is moistened. Now add minced apple into the batter. Spoon batter into the prepared muffin cups.
3. Bake in preheated range until lightly browned on the tops, about 25 minutes.

Preparing time 10 minutes, Total time 35 minutes, Servings: 1

VEGGIE SMOOTHIE

Nutritional Info: Calories: 118cal, Total fat: 0.5g, Saturated fat: 0.1g, Protein: 2.5g, Carbs: 34.5g, Sodium: 26mg, Fiber: 3.4g, Sugar: 11.3g

Ingredients

- ½ cup shredded cabbage
- 4 tbsp. chopped kale
- 4 tbsp. chopped spinach
- ½ cup chopped peeled apple
- 1 cup fresh lime juice
- 3cm ginger root, peeled and sliced

Instructions

1. In the high-power blender, gather all ingredients to it. Blend on high speed until ingredients turn into a smooth form.
2. Transfer into the serving glass. Serve and enjoy.

Preparing time 5 minutes, Total time 10 minutes, Servings: 1

Diabetes Cookbook

SPINACH EGG WHITE MUFFINS

Nutritional Info: Calories: 90cal, Total fat: 5g, Saturated fat: 3g, Protein: 10.3g, Carbs: 1g, Sodium: 186mg, Fiber: 0.2g, Sugar: 0.6g

Ingredients

- 4 tbsp. chopped spinach
- ¼ tsp. hot sauce
- Cooking spray
- Salt and ground black pepper
- 2 egg whites of small eggs
- 2 tbsp. shredded low-fat cheddar cheese

Instructions

1. Preheat range to 350 degrees Fahrenheit (175 degrees C). Spray the muffin's tin.
2. Combine egg whites, cheddar cheese, spinach, spicy sauce, salt, and pepper in a bowl. Fill each muffin cup ¾ full of the mixture.
3. Bake for 25 mins. Cool and serve.

Preparing time 5 minutes, Total time 30 minutes, Servings 1

TOFU SCRAMBLE

Nutritional Info: Calories: 225cal, Total fat: 12.2g, Saturated fat: 2.3g, Protein: 20.3g, Carbs: 14.5g, Sodium: 34mg, Fiber: 4.5g, Sugar: 8g

Ingredients

- 8 oz. firm tofu (drained)
- ½ cup seedless chopped tomato
- ½ cup seedless chopped green bell pepper
- ¼ cup chopped onion
- Salt and ground pepper to taste
- ½ tsp. ground garlic
- 1 tbsp. water
- ½ tsp olive oil

Instructions

1. Add oil to the pan and put it over moderate heat. Add chopped onions, bell pepper, and tomato to the pan, and cook for 3 minutes to soften. Crumble the tofu with a hand/fork and add to the pan; stir well.
2. In a small bowl, mix the spices. Add 1 tbsp of water to the sauces and mix, then pour into the tofu scramble and stir until everything is well-mixed. Cook for 5 minutes. Then serve and enjoy.

Preparing time 7 minutes, Total time 15 minutes, Servings 1

Diabetes Cookbook

FRENCH TOAST WITH BERRY COMPOTE

Nutritional Info: Calories: 93cal, Total fat: 1.4g, Saturated fat: 0.3g, Protein: 5g, Carbs: 17g, Sodium: 136mg, Fiber: 3g, Sugar: 3g

Ingredients

- Pinch of ground ginger
- 1 slice of whole-grain bread
- 3 tbsp. fresh blackberries or blueberries
- 1 small egg white
- Pinch of ground nutmeg
- Pinch of ground cinnamon

Instructions

1. Place half the berries in a bowl; mash into a juicy pulp. Transfer to a small saucepan with the remaining berries. Cook over low heat until warm, 3 to 5 minutes.
2. Beat egg whites, nutmeg, cinnamon, and ginger in a bowl. Dip bread in the mixture. Heat a skillet over medium heat. Cook the bread slice for 3 mins until light brown. Spoon the warm berry compote on top.

Preparing time 7 minutes, Total time 15 minutes, Servings 1

STRAWBERRY POWER PARFAIT

Nutritional Info: Calories: 267cal, Total fat: 2.7g, Saturated fat: 1.3g, Protein: 10.3g, Carbs: 52g, Sodium: 148mg, Fiber: 6.3g, Sugar: 28g

Ingredients

- ½ cup low-fat plain yogurt
- ½ tsp. cinnamon powder
- 1 small ripe banana
- ¾ cup strawberry
- ¼ cup grape nut cereal

Instructions

1. Place banana, yogurt, and cinnamon into the high-power blender and blend until smooth.
2. Transfer to the four-serving glass, and produce a layer of parfait, strawberry, and cereal to form the pattern.

Preparing time 5 minutes, Total time 5 minutes, Servings 1

BLUEBERRY-COCONUT PUDDING

Nutritional Info: Calories: 260cal, Total fat: 10g, Saturated fat: 5g Protein: 5g, Carbs: 39g, Sodium: 2mg, Fiber: 8g, Sugar: 2g

Ingredients

- ½ cup old-fashioned oats
- 2 tbsp. fresh blueberries
- 1 tbsp. chia seeds
- 1 cup unsweetened coconut milk
- ¼ tsp. lemon zest

Instructions

1. To the serving glass/jar, add oats, chia seeds, and coconut milk. Cover; shake to combine and refrigerate.
2. Top with lemon zest, chia seed, and blueberries to serve. Serve and enjoy.

Preparing time 5 minutes, Total time 35 minutes, Servings: 1

MIXED FRUIT COTTAGE CHEESE

Nutritional Info: Calories: 185cal, Total fat: 3g, Saturated fat: 1.5g, Protein: 17g, Carbs: 25g, Sodium: 459mg, Fiber: 5g, Sugar: 19g

Ingredients

- ½ cup low-fat cottage cheese
- 1 medium peach, wash and sliced
- ¼ cup fresh strawberry halved
- ¼ cup fresh raspberry

Instructions

1. In the serving bowl, add cottage cheese, and top it with peach slices, strawberry slices, and fresh raspberry. Stir well, serve, and enjoy.

Preparing time 5 minutes, Total time 5 minutes, Servings: 1

Diabetes Cookbook

SOUPS, GRAIN AND LEGUMES

CHILI CHICKEN SOUP WITH BLACK BEANS

Nutritional Info: Calories: 274cal, Total fat: 6g, Saturated fat: 1g
Protein: 22g, Carbs: 33g, Sodium: 561mg, Fiber: 6g, Sugar: 5g

Ingredients

- 80g chicken breasts cubed, without bone and skin
- ¼ cup chopped sweet red peppers
- 2 tbsp. chopped onion
- ½ tsp. olive oil
- 1 tbsp. chopped green chilies
- 1 tsp. minced garlic
- Pinch of ground coriander
- 3 oz. canned black beans, rinsed and drained
- 2½ oz. canned chopped tomatoes
- 4 tbsp. chicken broth
- 4 tbsp. water

Instructions

1. Add chicken, red peppers, and onion to a Dutch oven, put it over moderate heat, and cook for 5 minutes or until no longer pink. Then add green chilies, garlic, and coriander, and cook for a minute.
2. Now place in beans, tomatoes, broth, and water, and take a boil, stirring constantly. Add water if needed, decrease the stove heat to low, uncover, and cook for 15 minutes.

Preparing time 10 minutes, Total time 20 minutes, Servings: 1

TOMATO SOUP WITH LENTILS

Nutritional Info: Calories: 121cal, Total fat: 1g, Saturated fat: 0g
Protein: 8g, Carbs: 20g, Sodium: 351mg, Fiber: 9g, Sugar: 9g

Ingredients

- ¾ cup water
- 1 small carrot, sliced
- ¼ cup chopped onion
- 1½ tbsp. dried brown lentils, rinsed
- 2 tbsp. tomato paste
- 1 tsp. minced fresh parsley
- ½ tsp. white vinegar
- Pinch of garlic salt
- Pinch of black pepper

Instructions

1. Take water, carrots, onion, and lentils to a large saucepan, and boil over moderate heat. Decrease the stove heat to medium-low, cover, and cook for 20 to 25 minutes, or until the vegetables and lentils are tender.
2. Now add the remaining ingredients. Decrease the heat to low, uncover, and cook for 5 minutes to allow flavors to meld.

Preparing time 10 minutes, Total time 30 minutes, Servings: 1

Diabetes Cookbook

EASY TOMATO SOUP

Nutritional Info: Calories: 138cal, Total fat: 13g, Saturated fat: 6g
Protein: 4g, Carbs: 7g, Sodium: 503mg, Fiber: 1g, Sugar: 4g

Ingredients

- ½ tbsp. olive oil
- 1 tbsp. onion chopped
- 1 tsp. minced garlic
- Salt and black pepper to taste
- Pinch of dried oregano
- Pinch of dried basil
- 1½ tsp. tomato paste
- 5 tbsp. peeled and chopped tomatoes
- ½ cup water
- 1 tbsp. almond milk

Instructions

1. Put a large pan over moderate heat, add oil, and heat it. Add onion, garlic, and cook for 2 minutes. Place in tomatoes, salt, pepper, oregano, basil, tomato paste, and water. Bring to a boil, then lower to low heat.
2. Cook for 20 minutes on medium heat or until the tomatoes are tender and the sauce has thickened. Blend until smooth with an immersion blender. Cook more for a minute after adding the cream. If necessary, season with more salt. Warm the dish before serving.

Preparing time 5 minutes, Total time 25 minutes, Servings 1

ASPARAGUS SOUP

Nutritional Info: Calories: 56cal, Total fat: 3.2g, Saturated fat: 2.6g
Protein: 3g, Carbs: 5g, Sodium: 193mg, Fiber: 2g, Sugar: 2g

Ingredients

- ¼ cup chopped asparagus
- 2 tbsp. chopped red onion
- 3 tbsp. vegetable broth
- ½ tsp. coconut oil
- 1 tbsp. unsweetened coconut milk
- Salt and ground black pepper to taste
- Pinch of turmeric powder

Instructions

1. Add onion to the pan with coconut oil, and sauté over medium heat. Add salt and spices. When it's translucent, toss in the asparagus and cook for a few minutes. Add broth and boil. In a water bath, cool the vessel.
2. Add coconut milk to the immersion blender with the mixture, and blend until a smooth consistency is achieved. Serve the soup hot, garnished with a black pepper pinch to taste.

Preparing time 10 minutes, Total time 30 minutes, Servings 1

Diabetes Cookbook

CREAMY RICH AND CHICKEN SOUP

Nutritional Info: Calories: 312cal, Total fat: 9g, Saturated fat: 3g
Protein: 29g, Carbs: 26g, Sodium: 699mg, Fiber: 1g, Sugar: 6g

Ingredients

- 1 tsp. canola oil
- ½ small carrot, chopped
- 1 celery rib, chopped
- 2 tbsp. chopped onion
- ¼ tsp. minced garlic
- 1½ tbsp. long-grain rice
- Crushed black pepper to taste
- 110ml reduced-sodium chicken broth
- 3 tablespoons all-purpose flour
- 3 tbsp. low-fat milk
- ½ cup cooked chicken breast, cubed

Instructions

1. Add oil to a large pan, put it over medium-high heat, add carrots, celery, and onion, and cook until tender. Place in garlic, and cook for 1 minute, stirring constantly.
2. Now pour in the rice, seasonings, and broth, and take a boil. Decrease the stove heat to low, cover, and cook for 15 minutes, or until rice is tender. Stir flour and milk in a bowl, mix until smooth, then add to the soup.
3. Boil the soup, then cook and stir for 2 minutes, or until the sauce has thickened. In the end, add chicken and heat thoroughly.

Preparing time 10 minutes, Total time 30 minutes, Servings: 1

SALMON CHOWDER SOUP

Nutritional Info: Calories: 490cal, Total fat: 23g, Saturated fat: 13g
Protein: 39g, Carbs: 27g, Sodium: 1g, Fiber: 2g, Sugar: 8.6g

Ingredients

- 1 tsp. olive oil
- 1½ tbsp. chopped onion
- 1 tbsp. chopped celery
- Pinch of garlic powder
- ¼ cup peeled and diced potatoes
- ¼ diced carrots
- ¼ cup chicken broth
- Salt and ground black pepper
- ½ cup salmon
- 2 tbsp. evaporated milk
- 2 tbsp. low-fat half-and-half

Instructions

1. In a large pot, add oil, and put it over medium heat. Sauté the onion, celery, and garlic powder until the onions are soft. Add potatoes, carrots, broth, salt, pepper, and dill.
2. Boil the mixture, then remove the heat. Cover, and cook for 20 minutes. Pour in salmon, evaporated milk, and cheese. Cook until thoroughly heated.

Preparing time 15 minutes, Total time 30 minutes, Servings: 1

Diabetes Cookbook

TOFU AND SEAWEED SOUP

Nutritional Info: Calories: 44cal, Total fat: 2.5g, Saturated fat: 0.2g Protein: 2g, Carbs: 3g, Sodium: 232mg, Fiber: 0.4g, Sugar: 0.3g

Ingredients

- ½ tbsp. crumbled dried seaweed, soaked in water for 20 mins
- ½ tbsp. thinly sliced scallions
- ½ tsp. minced garlic
- ½ tsp. toasted sesame oil
- Ground black pepper
- ¾ cup water
- 50g diced firm tofu

Instructions

1. In a small bowl, add scallions, and garlic, with sesame oil and pepper. Take a medium saucepan over high heat. Cook, and keep stirring for a minute or until fragrant. Add the water and mix well.
2. Reduce the heat to medium-low to avoid boiling the liquid. Drain the seaweed and combine it with the tofu in the soup. Decrease the stove heat to medium-low and cook for about 10 minutes. Turn off the heat. If desired, season more with miso.

Preparing time 15 minutes, Total time 30 minutes, Servings 1

QUINOA BROWN RICE

Nutritional Info: Calories: 102cal, Total fat: 2g, Saturated fat: 0g Protein: 5g, Carbs: 16g, Sodium: 730mg, Fiber: 2g, Sugar: 1g

Ingredients

- 2½ tbsp. red quinoa
- 2½ tbsp. brown rice
- ½ cup + 2tbsp. low-sodium chicken broth

Instructions

1. Take chicken broth to the pan, and take a boil, then add the quinoa and rice. Stir lightly. Decrease the stove heat to low; cover and cook for 25 minutes.
2. When the grains have absorbed all the liquid, this is done. Then remove the pan and cover until ready to serve. Before adding this to a salad, let it cool to room temperature.

Preparing time 5 minutes, Total time 25 minutes, Servings 1

Diabetes Cookbook

BROWN RICE WITH MUSHROOM

Nutritional Info: Calories: 129cal, Total fat: 8g, Saturated fat: 1g
Protein: 3g, Carbs: 25g, Sodium: 10mg, Fiber: 2g, Sugar: 2.8g

Ingredients

- ¼ cup washed brown basmati rice
- 2 medium mushrooms, washed and sliced
- ¼ cup chopped onion
- ½ tbsp. olive oil
- ¼ green capsicum, sliced
- Black pepper and salt to taste
- ¾ cup water

Instructions

1. Add onions to a pan with olive oil. Sauté until the meat is pink. Toss in the mushrooms. Sauté until wilted. Add the sliced capsicum now. Add brown rice and continue to cook.
2. Cook for 5-7 minutes on medium-high heat. Add water, salt, and pepper, and cook for 15 minutes, or until the rice is cooked.

Preparing time 10 minutes, Total time 30 minutes, Servings: 1

BUCKWHEAT PANCAKE WITH BUTTERMILK

Nutritional Info: Calories: 238cal, Total fat: 11.6g, Saturated fat: 3g
Protein: 9.2g, Carbs: 25.5g, Sodium: 89mg, Fiber: 2g, Sugar: 2g

Ingredients

- 2 tbsp. buckwheat flour
- 2 tbsp. all-purpose flour
- ½ tsp. baking powder
- ½ tbsp. vegetable oil
- 1 small egg
- 2 tbsp. reduced-fat buttermilk

Instructions

1. Take a medium bowl, add flour with baking powder, and mix well. Stir in the vegetable oil, eggs, and buttermilk until thoroughly combined.
2. Place a skillet over moderate heat, and grease with nonstick cooking spray. Pour ¼ cup of batter onto a skillet for each pancake. Cook the pancakes for 2 mins on each side until golden brown. Serve and enjoy.

Preparing time 10 minutes, Total time 20 minutes, Servings: 1

Diabetes Cookbook

BARLEY RISOTTO WITH ZUCCHINIS AND TOMATOES

**Nutritional Info: Calories: 240cal, Total fat: 8g, Saturated fat: 1g
Protein: 10g, Carbs: 35g, Sodium: 417mg, Fiber: 7g, Sugar: 2g**

Ingredients

- 1 tsp. canola oil
- 1 tbsp. chopped shallot
- 3 tbsp. pearled barley
- ½ cup vegetable stock
- 1 tbsp. dry white wine
- ¼ cup sliced zucchini
- ¼ cup chopped tomato
- Salt and ground black pepper to taste

Instructions

1. In a pressure cooker, add canola oil, and heat it. Add shallot and barley and cook for 3 minutes. Add the stock and wine to the cooker, cover, and set the pressure to high. Cook at high pressure for 15–20 minutes.
2. If the risotto still has a soupy texture, uncover it; cook it for a few minutes longer until the liquid has been reduced. Add in zucchini and tomato. Sprinkle with salt and pepper.

Preparing time 20 minutes, Total time 45 minutes, Servings: 1

RAVA UPMA

**Nutritional Info: Calories: 261cal, Total fat: 5.6g, Saturated fat: 0.7g
Protein: 8.6g, Carbs: 44.6g, Sodium: 16mg, Fiber: 6g, Sugar: 4g**

Ingredients

- 1 tsp. oil
- ½ tsp. mustard seeds
- 1 tsp. urad dal
- ½ cup chopped onion
- ¼ cup chopped jalapeno pepper
- 2 tbsp. chopped coriander leaves
- Salt to taste
- ¼ cup chopped cauliflower
- ¼ cup couscous or semolina

Instructions

1. Cook couscous in a hot pack container by pouring boiling water over it. When done, set it aside. Add cauliflower florets to the high-power food blender until they are the consistency of rice.
2. Add oil to the pan. Add mustard seeds and let them pop. Stir in the urad dal, green chilies, and onions. Allow for a few minutes of browning. Toss in the cauliflower 'rice' and stir for a few minutes. Cook the couscous, add salt and pepper, and garnish with coriander leaves.

Preparing time 5 minutes, Total time 20 minutes, Servings: 1

Diabetes Cookbook

BLACK BEAN SOUP

**Nutritional Info: Calories: 170cal, Total fat: 3.5g, Saturated fat: 0.5g
Protein: 20g, Carbs: 15g, Sodium: 420mg, Fiber: 5g, Sugar: 4g**

Ingredients

- ½ tsp. olive oil
- 1 tbsp. chopped onion
- 70g chicken breast, without skin and bone
- Black pepper to taste
- 70g fire-roasted canned tomatoes
- ½ tsp. chili powder
- 1½ tbsp. frozen corn
- 60g canned black or red beans (rinsed and drained)
- 160ml low-sodium chicken broth

Instructions

1. Grease the large soup pot with cooking spray. Sauté the onion and oil for 3 minutes over medium-high heat or until clear. Season the chicken with salt and pepper.
2. Cook the chicken for about 7 minutes or until the chicken is slightly browned. Place in leftover ingredients, decrease the stove heat to low, and cook for 15 minutes.

Preparing time 10 minutes, Total time 25 minutes, Servings: 1

BEAN WITH BROWN RICE

**Nutritional Info: Calories: 334cal, Total fat: 6g, Saturated fat: 2g
Protein: 11g, Carbs: 59g, Sodium: 444mg, Fiber: 4g, Sugar: 2g**

Ingredients

- 3 tbsp. canned black beans, rinsed, and drained
- 3 tbsp. jarred thick and chunky mild salsa
- 1 tbsp. canned no-salt-added corn, drained
- ½ cup cooked brown rice

Instructions

1. Add black beans, salsa, and corn to a saucepan, and put it over medium heat until bubbly (nearly 10 minutes).
2. Over 1/2 cup hot, cooked rice, spoon 1/2 cup bean mixture. Serve and have fun.

Preparing time 15 minutes, Total time 25 minutes, Servings: 1

Diabetes Cookbook

CHICKEN AND BLACK BEAN BURRITOS

Nutritional Info: Calories: 370cal, Total fat: 14g, Saturated fat: 3g Protein: 37g, Carbs: 36g, Sodium: 500mg, Fiber: 19g, Sugar: 4g

Ingredients

- ¼ mashed avocado
- 1 large low-carb whole wheat tortilla
- 2 tbsp. salsa
- ½ cup shredded cooked chicken breast
- ¼ cup black beans, rinsed and drained
- 1½ tbsp. low-fat shredded cheddar cheese
- ¼ cup shredded lettuce
- ¼ cup chopped tomatoes

Instructions

1. Spread mashed avocado on a tortilla. Top with salsa, chicken, black beans, cheese, lettuce, and diced tomatoes.
2. Fold into the burrito. Serve and enjoy.

Preparing time 5 minutes, Total time 10 minutes, Servings 1

WHITE BEAN CHICKEN CHILI

Nutritional Info: Calories: 239cal, Total fat: 2.9g, Saturated fat: 0.4g Protein: 21.7g, Carbs: 31.7g, Sodium: 582mg, Fiber: 10g, Sugar: 5g

Ingredients

- 160g canned white beans, without liquid and salt
- ½ cup reduced-sodium chicken broth
- 60g chicken breast halves, without skin and bone
- ¼ cup finely chopped onions
- 3 tbsp. chopped yellow sweet peppers
- 1 oz. canned diced green chili peppers
- 1 tsp. minced garlic
- ½ tsp. ground cumin
- Pinch of crushed dried oregano
- Salt and cayenne pepper to taste
- 1 tbsp. fat-free plain Greek yogurt
- 1 tbsp. freshly chopped cilantro leaves

Instructions

1. Add all ingredients to the 4- to 5-quart slow cooker except yogurt and cilantro. Cover, and cook on low for 4 to 5 hours or high for 2 to 3 hours.
2. When done, take the chicken to the dish and shred it with two forks. Put back the chicken into the pressure cooker to heat thoroughly. Top with yogurt and cilantro, if desired.

Preparing time 15 minutes, Total time 3 hours, Servings 1

Diabetes Cookbook

BAKED BEANS

Nutritional Info: Calories: 234cal, Total fat: 0.9g, Saturated fat: 0.3g Protein: 16g, Carbs: 43g, Sodium: 223mg, Fiber: 13.4g, Sugar: 3g

Ingredients

- 2 tbsp. tomato sauce
- ¼ tsp. prepared yellow mustard
- ¼ tsp. Worcestershire sauce
- ½ can white beans, rinsed and drained
- 2 tbsp. chopped onion
- 1 tbsp. Hormel bacon bits

Instructions

1. Add tomato sauce, mustard, and Worcestershire sauce to the slow cooker, then stir in great northern beans. Toss in the onion and bacon bits.
2. To combine, whisk everything together thoroughly. Cover, and cook on low heat for 7 hours or high for 2½ to 3 hours, stirring occasionally.

Preparing time 15 minutes, Total time 3 hours, Servings: 1

RED LENTILS STEW

Nutritional Info: Calories: 404cal, Total fat: 23.6g, Saturated fat: 3.8g Protein: 14g, Carbs: 36g, Sodium: 274mg, Fiber: 16.4g, Sugar: 4g

Ingredients

- ¼ cup red lentils, rinsed and soaked in water for 40 mins
- 1¼ cup hot boiling water
- ¾ tsp. salt
- Black pepper to taste
- 2 tbsp. margarine
- 6 tbsp. crushed canned tomato
- ¼ cup chopped onion
- ¾ tsp. dill seeds
- ¾ tsp. minced garlic
- 1 bay leaves

Instructions

1. Drain the lentils, add them with the other ingredients in a microwave-safe bowl, cover, and cook on high for 15 minutes.
2. Remove the bowl, stir well, cover, and microwave for another 45-60 minutes on medium. Allow the stew to rest for an hour. When you're ready to serve, reheat the dish.

Preparing time 10 minutes, Total time 1 hour 20 minutes, Servings: 1

Diabetes Cookbook

CHICKPEA STEW WITH SPINACH

**Nutritional Info: Calories: 380cal, Total fat: 11g, Saturated fat: 1.8g
Protein: 20g, Carbs: 48g, Sodium: 176mg, Fiber: 11g, Sugar: 3g**

Ingredients

- 3 oz. dried chickpeas, soaked overnight in water
- 2 ½ oz. frozen spinach, thawed
- ¼ cup onions
- ½ garlic cloves
- ½ sprigs of rosemary, rinse, and pluck the needles.
- ¼ cup halved tomatoes
- ½ tbsps. olive oil
- 1 bay leave
- Pinch of chili powder

Instructions

1. Take the large pot, add oil, and heat it over medium temperature; add the onions and garlic and cook until soft. Simmer chickpeas with 1½ cups of water, rosemary, bay leaves, and chili powder for 35 minutes.
2. In the end, add tomato and spinach, and cook more for 15 minutes. Remove the bay leaves before serving.

Preparing time 10 minutes, Total time 1 hour, Servings 1

CHICKPEA CURRY WITH SWEET POTATO

**Nutritional Info: Calories: 380cal, Total fat: 21.6g, Saturated fat: 13.4g
Protein: 5g, Carbs: 22g, Sodium: 515mg, Fiber: 5g, Sugar: 3.4g**

Ingredients

- ½ tbsp. olive oil
- 2 tbsp. chopped onion
- 1 tsp. minced garlic
- ¼ tsp. minced fresh ginger root
- 5 tbsp. canned chickpeas, drained
- 4 tbsp. canned diced tomatoes
- 3½ tbsp. canned coconut milk
- ½ small sweet potato, cubed
- Pinch of ground turmeric
- Salt and pepper to taste
- 2 ½ tbsp. baby spinach

Instructions

1. Add onion, garlic, and ginger to a skillet, put it over medium heat, and sauté until softened, about 5 minutes. Then add chickpeas, tomatoes, coconut milk, and sweet potato, and boil the mixture.
2. Decrease the stove heat to low heat; sauté until the vegetables are tender, about 15 minutes. Sprinkle garam masala, salt, and pepper to taste. Just before serving, toss in the spinach.

Preparing time 10 minutes, Total time 30 minutes, Servings 1

Diabetes Cookbook

YELLOW LENTIL CURRY

**Nutritional Info: Calories: 261cal, Total fat: 10.7g, Saturated fat: 1.8g
Protein: 12.7g, Carbs: 29g, Sodium: 5mg, Fiber: 12.7g, Sugar: 1.7g**

Ingredients

- 2 tbsp. red lentils
- 2 tbsp. yellow mung bean
- Pinch of turmeric powder
- 1 cup water
- Salt to taste
- ¾ tbsp. peanut oil (peanut oil)
- Pinch of cumin powder
- ½ red chili peppers flacks
- ½ tsp. minced garlic

Instructions

1. Place lentils with mung in a pan with turmeric and water and bring to a boil. Then cover and cook for 40–45 minutes on low heat. Add salt and pepper.
2. In a frying pan, heat the oil and fry the cumin, chilies, and garlic until the chilies darken. Place the cooked beans and lentils in a bowl and serve on plates. If desired, garnish with chilies.

Preparing time 15 minutes, Total time 60 minutes, Servings 1

SPICY BLACK CHICKPEA STEW

**Nutritional Info: Calories: 260cal, Total fat: 16.8g, Saturated fat: 2.1g
Protein: 7.2g, Carbs: 24.4g, Sodium: 179mg, Fiber: 6.9g, Sugar: 5.6g**

Ingredients

- ½ cup black chickpeas, soaked in water overnight in water
- ½ cup chopped onion
- ½ tsp. mustard seeds
- Pinch of turmeric powder
- 1 cup water
- ½ tsp red chili powder
- ½ tsp. garam masala powder
- ½ tsp. coriander powder
- Salt to taste
- 1 tbsp. olive oil

Instructions

1. Add 1½ cups of water with soaked chickpeas to pressure cooker and cook till 7-8 whistle. In a pan, add and heat oil. Add mustard seeds and let them crackle. Add turmeric powder with onions and sauté the onions till they are translucent and cooked properly.
2. Add coriander and garam masala powder with red chili powder and mix well. Add the cooked chickpeas (only chickpea) and salt and mix them well. Add the half cup of water, cover the pan, and let the chickpeas cook on steam for 3-4minutes. Stir occasionally.

Preparing time 15 minutes, Total time 25 minutes, Servings

Diabetes Cookbook

SWEET AND CREAMY CORN

**Nutritional Info: Calories: 131cal, Total fat: 4g, Saturated fat: 1g
Protein: 3g, Carbs: 20.8g, Sodium: 100mg, Fiber: 2g, Sugar: 2g**

Ingredients

- ½ cup frozen whole-kernel corn, thawed
- 1 tbsp. low-fat light sour cream
- ½ tbsp. buttery spread
- ¼ tsp. Dijon Mustard
- Pinch of black pepper

Instructions

1. In a skillet, add corn, put it on moderate heat, and cook for 2 to 3 minutes, or until heated through. Add the leftover ingredients.
2. Cook for a half minute, or until just bubbly, constantly stirring (do not boil). Remove from heat, cover; keep aside for 3 minutes to allow flavors to meld.

Preparing time 5 minutes, Total time 10 minutes, Servings: 1

CORN FRITTERS

**Nutritional Info: Calories: 180cal, Total fat: 5.6g, Saturated fat: 0.6g
Protein: 8g, Carbs: 26g, Sodium: 357mg, Fiber: 2g, Sugar: 4g**

Ingredients

- ¾ cup corn frozen or fresh
- 2 tbsp. all-purpose flour
- 1/8 tsp. baking soda
- 1/8 tsp. onion powder
- 1 dash of cayenne pepper
- 1/8 tsp. garlic powder
- Salt and black pepper to taste
- 1 large egg white, lightly beaten
- 2 tbsp. low-fat milk
- 1 tsp. canola oil

Instructions

1. Add corn, flour, baking soda, spices, salt, and pepper to a large bowl. Stir in egg white and milk. In a skillet, add oil, and put it over medium heat.
2. Drop half of the batter onto a hot skillet to make each fritter. To make the fritters thinner, press the batter down a little. Cook for about 4 mins per side. Serve and have fun.

Preparing time 5 minutes, Total time 10 minutes, Servings: 1

Diabetes Cookbook

SNACKS AND SANDWICHES

GRANOLA

**Nutritional Info: Calories: 194cal, Total fat: 7.9g, Saturated fat: 0.8g
Protein: 2.5g, Carbs: 29.5g, Sodium: 29mg, Fiber: 2.5g, Sugar: 3.5g**

Ingredients

- ½ tbsp. agave nectar
- ½ tbsp. canola oil
- 2-3 drops of vanilla extract
- 3 tbsp. rolled oats
- 2¼ tsp. chopped pecans
- ¼ tsp. ground cinnamon
- Pinch of salt

Instructions

1. To preheat the oven, set the range to 325 degrees Fahrenheit. Place parchment paper to arrange the rimmed baking sheet. In a bowl, add nectar, oil, and vanilla extract. Combine the oats, pecans, cinnamon, and salt.
2. Spread out evenly on the baking sheet that has been prepared. Bake the granola for 10 to 15 minutes, stirring halfway through. Before storing, allow cooling completely.

Preparing time: 5 minutes, Total time 20 minutes, Servings: 1

CINNAMON OATMEAL COOKIES WITH RAISINS

**Nutritional Info: Calories: 273cal, Total fat: 10g, Saturated fat: 1.9g
Protein: 5g, Carbs: 45g, Sodium: 74mg, Fiber: 1g, Sugar: 7.8g**

Ingredients

- 3 tbsp. whole-wheat flour
- ¼ tsp. baking powder
- Big pinch of ground cinnamon
- Salt to taste
- 1½ tbsp. monk fruit sweetener
- 1 tbsp. cashew butter softened
- 1 small egg whites
- 2-3 drops of vanilla extract
- 2½ tbsp. old-fashioned rolled oats
- 1¼ tbsp. raisins

Instructions

1. Preheat the oven range to 350 degrees F. Lightly coat a baking sheet with cooking spray. Add flour, baking powder, ground cinnamon, and salt to a bowl. Mix sugar, butter, egg, and vanilla in the other bowl.
2. Stir in the flour mixture, oats, and raisins with a wooden spoon until everything is well combined. Drop 1 tablespoon of batter onto the prepared baking sheet. Bake for 12 to 14 minutes, or until golden brown on the bottom.

Preparing time: 5 minutes, Total time 20 minutes, Servings: 1

Diabetes Cookbook

CUCUMBER SANDWICH

**Nutritional Info: Calories: 147cal, Total fat: 4g, Saturated fat: 2g
Protein: 1.5g, Carbs: 20g, Sodium: 74mg, Fiber: 1g, Sugar: 7.8g**

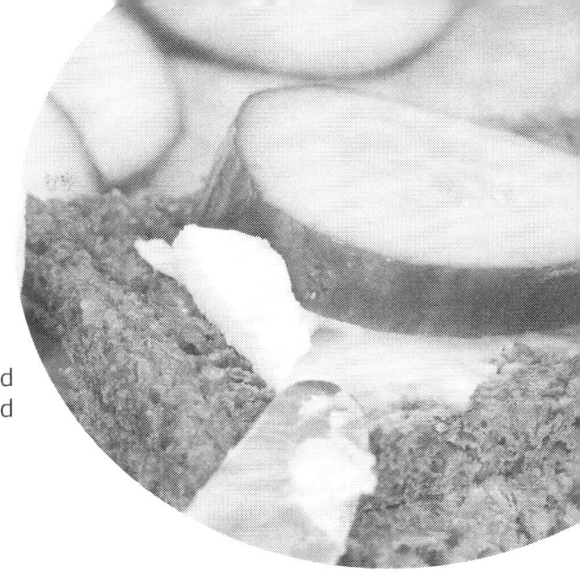

Ingredients

- 1 slice of whole-grain bread
- 1 tbsp. goat cheese
- 1 small cucumber, sliced
- Salt and ground pepper

Instructions

1. Spread goat cheese on the bread slice and top with cucumber slices. Sprinkle salt and pepper as per your taste. Serve and enjoy.

Preparing time 5 minutes, Total time 5 minutes, Servings 1

ENERGY BALLS

**Nutritional Info: Calories: 282cal, Total fat: 13g, Saturated fat: 2.3g
Protein: 8g, Carbs: 28g, Sodium: 48mg, Fiber: 2g, Sugar: 2.3g**

Ingredients

- 3½ tbsp. rolled oats
- 1 tbsp natural peanut butter
- ½ tbsp. agave nectar
- 1 tsp. mini chocolate chips
- 1 tsp. unsweetened shredded coconut

Instructions

1. Add oats, peanut butter, agave nectar, chocolate chips, and coconut to a bowl, and stir well.
2. Take a tablespoon and roll the mixture into balls. Serve immediately or keep in the fridge to chill.

Preparing time 5 minutes, Total time 5 minutes, Servings 1

Diabetes Cookbook

CARROT ENERGY BALLS

Nutritional Info: Calories: 295cal, **Total fat:** 4g, **Saturated fat:** 0.2g **Protein:** 14g, **Carbs:** 30g, **Sodium:** 30mg, **Fiber:** 1.6g, **Sugar:** 5g

Ingredients

- 25g pitted and roughly dates
- 6½g old-fashioned rolled oats
- 1 tsp. chopped pecans
- 1 tsp. chia seeds
- 1½ tbsp. chopped carrots
- Pinch of ground cinnamon
- Pinch of ginger powder
- Pinch of turmeric powder
- Salt and ground black pepper

Instructions

1. In a food blender, add dates, oats, pecans, and chia seeds; pulse until well chopped. Add carrots, cinnamon, ginger, turmeric, salt, and pepper, and combine thoroughly.
2. Using a scant 1 tbsp of the mixture, roll into balls. Serve and enjoy.

Preparing time 15 minutes, Total time 15 minutes, Servings: 1

CAPRESE SKEWERS

Nutritional Info: Calories: 54cal, **Total fat:** 3.3g, **Saturated fat:** 1.6g **Protein:** 2.8g, **Carbs:** 3.2g, **Sodium:** 217mg, **Fiber:** 0.2g, **Sugar:** 0.4g

Ingredients

- 2 fresh and small low-fat cottage cheese balls
- 2 cherry tomatoes
- 3 fresh basil leaves
- Salt & ground pepper to taste

Instructions

1. Thread cottage cheese, basil, and cherry tomatoes on small skewers as your desired patron.
2. Sprinkle salt and pepper and serve immediately.

Preparing time 10 minutes, Total time 10 minutes, Servings: 1

Diabetes Cookbook

DATE & PISTACHIO BALLS

Nutritional Info: Calories: 174cal, Total fat: 6g, Saturated fat: 1.6g
Protein: 3g, Carbs: 27.5g, Sodium: 0.8mg, Fiber: 1.4g, Sugar: 10.7g

Ingredients

- 22g pitted and chopped whole dates
- 10g chopped raw unsalted pistachios, shelled
- 10g golden raisins
- 1/8 teaspoon ground fennel seeds

Instructions

1. Add dates, pistachios, raisins, fennel, and in a food blender. Process until the mixture is finely chopped.
2. Use about 1 tablespoon per ball. Roll between the hands. Chill or serve immediately.

Preparing time 10 minutes, Total time 10 minutes, Servings 1

AIR-FRIED SWEET POTATO CHIPS

Nutritional Info: Calories: 97cal, Total fat: 4.4g, Saturated fat: 0.2g
Protein: 1.26g, Carbs: 13g, Sodium: 39mg, Fiber: 2g, Sugar: 5g

Ingredients

- 1 small sweet potato, sliced, boiled in water for 20 mins
- ½ tsp. canola oil
- Salt and ground white pepper

Instructions

1. In a bowl, add sweet potato, oil, salt, and pepper; gently toss to coat. Cooking sprays the air-fryer basket lightly. Place chips in 1 layer in the basket.
2. Cook for 10 minutes at 350 degrees F until crispy, then flip and cook more for 5 minutes. Then remove; set it aside. Allow 5 minutes for the chips to cool before serving.

Preparing time 25 minutes, Total time 45 minutes, Servings 1

Diabetes Cookbook

DRY FRUIT BITS

Nutritional Info: Calories: 225cal, Total fat: 11g, Saturated fat: 1.8g, Protein: 8g, Carbs: 23.6g, Sodium: 4mg, Fiber: 4g, Sugar: 14g

Ingredients

- 10g chopped almonds
- 15g dried figs
- 19g dried apricots
- 2 tbsp. shredded coconut, unsweetened

Instructions

1. Add almonds, figs, and apricots to a food blender; process until finely chopped.
2. Take out the small amount of mixture, shape them into small balls, then dredge in coconut. Serve and enjoy.

Preparing time: 10 minutes, Total time: 10 minutes, Servings: 1

ZUCCHINI MUFFINS

Nutritional Info: Calories: 297cal, Total fat: 25g, Saturated fat: 12g, Protein: 10g, Carbs: 13g, Sodium: 120mg, Fiber: 3g, Sugar: 4g

Ingredients

- ¼ cup almond flour
- Salt to taste
- ¼ tsp. baking powder
- 1 tbsp. coconut oil
- 1 tsp. agave nectar
- 1 medium egg white
- 2 tbsp. shredded zucchini

Instructions

1. To preheat, set the oven range to 350F. Arrange 2 paper liners for large or regular cupcake pans; set aside. Add baking powder, almond flour, and salt to a bowl. Mix in the coconut oil, agave nectar, and egg white until everything is well combined.
2. Add the shredded zucchini and mix well. Fill your paper liners halfway with batter. Bake for 20 minutes. Allow 5 minutes to cool before serving.

Preparing time: 10 minutes, Total time: 35 minutes, Servings: 1

Diabetes Cookbook

OAT, GINGER, AND APRICOT ENERGY BALLS

Nutritional Info: Calories: 140cal, Total fat: 6g, Saturated fat: 2.8g
Protein: 2g, Carbs: 16g, Sodium: 14mg, Fiber: 2g, Sugar: 3g

Ingredients

- 12g dried apricots
- 1 tsp. rolled oats
- 1 tsp. shredded unsweetened coconut
- 1 tsp. tahini
- 1 tsp. agave nectar
- 1/8 tsp. ginger powder
- Pinch of salt

Instructions

1. In a food processor, combine apricots, oats, coconut, tahini, agave, ginger, and salt. Pulse until finely chopped or until the mixture is crumbly but can be pressed to form a cohesive ball.
2. With wet hands, squeeze about 1 tablespoon of the mixture tightly between your hands and roll it into a ball. Serve and enjoy.

Preparing time 10 minutes, Total time 35 minutes, Servings:

AIR FRIED ZUCCHINI CHIPS

Nutritional Info: Calories: 225cal, Total fat: 14.3g, Saturated fat: 2.8g
Protein: 14g, Carbs: 10g, Sodium: 195mg, Fiber: 4.2g, Sugar: 3.2g

Ingredients

- 1 small zucchini, thinly sliced
- ¼ cup almond flour
- 2 tbsp. grated parmesan cheese
- 1/8 tsp. garlic powder
- Salt and ground black pepper to taste
- 1 small egg white, beaten

Instructions

1. Set the air fryer range to 350 degrees F. Add almond flour, garlic powder, salt, pepper, and parmesan cheese to a small bowl.
2. To coat zucchini slices, dip them in egg white mixture and almond flour. Arrange zucchini chips in a single layer in the fryer basket. Cook for a total of 8-10 minutes.

Preparing time 10 minutes, Total time 20 minutes, Servings: 1

Diabetes Cookbook

CRISPY CHICKPEAS

Nutritional Info: Calories: 132cal, Total fat: 5.8g, Saturated fat: 0.7g
Protein: 4.7g, Carbs: 11.5g, Sodium: 86mg, Fiber: 3.4g, Sugar: 3.2g

Ingredients

- ¼ cup canned unsalted chickpeas, rinsed, drained, and pat dries
- 1 tsp. toasted sesame oil
- Pinch of smoked paprika
- Pinch of crushed red pepper
- Pinch of salt
- 1 tsp. lime juice

Instructions

1. Add chickpeas and oil with paprika, crushed red pepper, and salt to taste in a bowl. Coat the fryer basket with cooking spray.
2. Cook, shaking the basket occasionally, at 400 degrees F until very well browned, 12 to 14 minutes. Serve with lime wedges squeezed over the chickpeas.

Preparing time 10 minutes, Total time 20 minutes, Servings: 1

VEGGIE & HUMMUS SANDWICH

Nutritional Info: Calories: 396cal, Total fat: 16.5g, Saturated fat: 0.7g
Protein: 14g, Carbs: 48g, Sodium: 407mg, Fiber: 12g, Sugar: 2g

Ingredients

- 2 slices of whole-grain bread
- 3 tbsp. hummus
- 2 tbsp. mashed avocado
- ½ cup mixed salad greens
- 2 tbsp. sliced bell pepper
- ½ small cucumber, sliced
- 4 tbsp. shredded carrot

Instructions

1. Place the mashed avocado on one piece of bread and spread hummus on the other.
2. Put some greens, red bell pepper, cucumber, and carrot in the sandwich. Cut in half and serve immediately.

Preparing time 10 minutes, Total time 10 minutes, Servings: 1

Diabetes Cookbook

PITA SANDWICH WITH SALMON

**Nutritional Info: Calories: 239cal, Total fat: 7.1g, Saturated fat: 1.4g
Protein: 24.8g, Carbs: 19g, Sodium: 510mg, Fiber: 2.3g, Sugar: 3g**

Ingredients

- ½ 6-inch whole-wheat pita bread
- 2 tbsp. non-fat yogurt
- 2 tsp. chopped fresh dill
- 2 tsp. lemon juice
- ½ tsp. prepared horseradish
- 3 oz. canned flaked salmon, drained

Instructions

1. Combine non-fat yogurt, dill, and lemon juice in a small bowl; stir in salmon. Stuff the pita half with the salmon salad and fresh dill.

Preparing time 10 minutes, Total time 10 minutes, Servings 1

STRAWBERRY & CREAM CHEESE SANDWICH

**Nutritional Info: Calories: 191cal, Total fat: 5g, Saturated fat: 1.7g
Protein: 8g, Carbs: 28.5g, Sodium: 200mg, Fiber: 2.5g, Sugar: 4.7g**

Ingredients

- 1 tbsp. low-fat cream cheese
- ¼ tsp. agave nectar
- Pinch of freshly grated orange zest
- 2 whole-wheat sandwich bread slices
- 2 strawberries, sliced

Instructions

1. Combine cream cheese, agave nectar, and orange zest in a bowl. Spread cheese mixture over the bread. Place strawberry slices on one piece of bread, and top with the other. Serve and enjoy.

Preparing time 5 minutes, Total time 5 minutes, Servings 1

Diabetes Cookbook

SAUTEED FRESH CORN WITH HERBS

**Nutritional Info: Calories: 172cal, Total fat: 5g, Saturated fat: 3g
Protein: 3g, Carbs: 31g, Sodium: 121mg, Fiber: 3g, Sugar: 3g**

Ingredients

- 1 cup of fresh corn
- 1 tsp. unsalted butter
- Salt and ground black pepper
- ¼ tsp. freshly chopped coriander

Instructions

1. Add butter to the large skillet and put it over medium heat. Sautee the corn with the salt, pepper, and coriander for about 10 minutes, until nice and brown.

Preparing time 5 minutes, Total time 15 minutes, Servings 1

Diabetes Cookbook

SALADS AND SIDES

PERFECT COBB SALAD

Nutritional Info: Calories: 329cal, Total fat: 15.3g, Saturated fat: 4.3g Protein: 31g, Carbs: 17g, Sodium: 452mg, Fiber: 6g, Sugar: 2.9g

Ingredients

- 4 cherry tomatoes, halved or quartered
- ½ small avocado, peeled and sliced
- 1 medium egg, hard-boiled
- 2 cups mixed green salad
- 2 oz. cooked chopped chicken breast
- 1 oz. low-fat cottage cheese, crumbled

Instructions

1. In a salad bowl or plate, add mixed greens. Place in chicken, avocado, sliced egg, cherry tomatoes, and cottage cheese crumbles in a mixing bowl. Mix them, serve, and enjoy.

Preparing time 5 minutes, Total time 5 minutes, Servings 1

SPINACH SMOOTHIE

Nutritional Info: Calories: 328cal, Total fat: 13g, Saturated fat: 2g Protein: 16g, Carbs: 36.8g, Sodium: 60mg, Fiber: 9g, Sugar: 19

Ingredients

- 1 cup unsweetened soy milk
- 1 cup freshly chopped spinach
- 1 small fresh banana
- 1 tbsp. natural peanut butter

Instructions

1. In the high-power blender, add all ingredients to it. Blend them well until all the elements turn into smooth form.
2. Transfer it to the serving jar/glass. Serve and enjoy.

Preparing time 5 minutes, Total time 5 minutes, Servings 1

Diabetes Cookbook

SHREDDED CARROT AND RAISIN SALAD

**Nutritional Info: Calories: 157cal, Total fat: 7g, Saturated fat: 1.8g
Protein: 1.5g, Carbs: 22g, Sodium: 239mg, Fiber: 6g, Sugar: 2.9g**

Ingredients

- ½ tbsp. extra-virgin olive oil
- ½ tbsp. lemon juice
- ¼ tsp. Dijon mustard
- Pinch of salt
- Pinch of ground black pepper
- 1 small carrot, coarsely shredded
- 1½ tbsp. raisins

Instructions

1. Add oil, lemon juice, mustard, salt, and pepper to a large bowl; stir until well mixed.
2. Add carrots and raisins; toss to combine. Set aside for 30 minutes to chill or serve immediately.

Preparing time 5 minutes, Total time 5 minutes, Servings 1

CHEESY CASSEROLE

**Nutritional Info: Calories: 264cal, Total fat: 17g, Saturated fat: 4g
Protein: 20g, Carbs: 7.8g, Sodium: 179mg, Fiber: 4g, Sugar: 3g**

Ingredients

- 2 large eggs
- 1 tbsp. low-fat milk
- ½ serving of cauliflower tots (2 tots total)
- 2 tbsp. cheddar cheese
- 2 tbsp. canned mushrooms slices

Instructions

1. Grease a casserole dish. Preheat the oven to 450. Toss all the ingredients together in a stand mixer until well combined.
2. Pour the mixture into a casserole dish and bake for 20-25 minutes.

Preparing time 5 minutes, Total time 30 minutes, Servings 1

Diabetes Cookbook

STRIPED CUCUMBER SALAD

Nutritional Info: Calories: 84cal, **Total fat:** 4g, **Saturated fat:** 0.4g
Protein: 3g, **Carbs:** 5g, **Sodium:** 3.5mg, **Fiber:** 1.3g, **Sugar:** 2.6g

Ingredients

- 1 small cucumber
- 1 tbsp. rice vinegar
- Salt and pepper to taste
- ½ tbsp. toasted sesame seeds

Instructions

1. Peel cucumbers to leave alternating green stripes. Cut cucumbers in half lengthwise, and the seeds scoop out with a spoon. Cut into very thin slices with a food processor or a sharp knife. Pat the strips dry completely.
2. In a medium mixing bowl, combine the vinegar and salt and stir to dissolve. Toss in the cucumbers and sesame seeds to combine. Serve immediately.

Preparing time 6 minutes, Total time 6 minutes, Servings: 1

MUSHROOM GRAVY

Nutritional Info: Calories: 105cal, **Total fat:** 5g, **Saturated fat:** 1g
Protein: 6g, **Carbs:** 9g, **Sodium:** 172mg, **Fiber:** 1g, **Sugar:** 0.9g

Ingredients

- ¼ tsp. canola oil
- 2 tbsp. sliced fresh mushrooms
- 1 tsp. minced garlic
- 1 oz. turkey gravy
- 1 tsp. chopped parsley
- 2 tbsp. chicken broth

Instructions

1. In a large nonstick skillet, add oil, and put it over medium-high heat. Toss in the mushrooms. Cook, frequently stirring, for 6 minutes, or until lightly browned.
2. Now add garlic and cook for 15 seconds. Add gravy; cook until the gravy is thoroughly heated. Add parsley, and thin the gravy with water (if needed). Serve with a side of rice.

Preparing time 5 minutes, Total time 11 minutes, Servings: 1

Diabetes Cookbook

ARUGULA CITRUS SALAD

**Nutritional Info: Calories: 222cal, Total fat: 14.3g, Saturated fat: 1.8g
Protein: 2.8g, Carbs: 20.7g, Sodium: 241mg, Fiber: 4.9g, Sugar: 15g**

Ingredients

- 1 small beet, peeled and sliced
- 1 small orange, peeled and segments
- ¾ cup packed baby arugula
- ½ tbsp. lime juice
- ½ tbsp. extra-virgin olive oil
- Salt and black pepper to taste

Instructions

1. Add orange, arugula, lime juice, oil, beet slices, and salt to a medium bowl. Toss until well combined. Serve and enjoy.

Preparing time 10 minutes, Total time 10 minutes, Servings 1

GRILLED EGGPLANT

**Nutritional Info: Calories: 88cal, Total fat: 7g, Saturated fat: 0g
Protein: 1g, Carbs: 6.7g, Sodium: 152mg, Fiber: 4g, Sugar: 3g**

Ingredients

- 1 small eggplant, sliced
- 1 tbsp. olive oil
- ½ tbsp. lime juice
- ¼ tsp. Cajun seasoning

Instructions

1. Brush eggplant slices with oil. Drizzle with lime juice; sprinkle with Cajun seasoning. Let stand for 5 minutes.
2. Cover, and grill eggplant, over medium heat until tender, 4-5 minutes per side.

Preparing time 10 minutes, Total time 20 minutes, Servings 1

Diabetes Cookbook

CARROT AND CUCUMBER SALAD

**Nutritional Info: Calories: 92cal, Total fat: 4.9g, Saturated fat: 0g
Protein: 1.6g, Carbs: 10.8g, Sodium: 39mg, Fiber: 2.8g, Sugar: 6g**

Ingredients

- 1 tbsp. rice wine vinegar
- ¾ tsp. toasted sesame oil
- Salt to taste
- Pinch of chipotle chili powder
- 1/4 cup chopped cilantro
- Pinch of black pepper
- 1 small cucumber, sliced
- 1 small carrot, julienned
- 2 tbsp. sliced onion

Instructions

1. Add vinegar, cilantro, oil, salt, chili powder, and black pepper. Stir in cucumber, carrots, and red onion.
2. Toss to coat evenly. Cover; refrigerate for 2 to 4 hours before serving. Then serve and enjoy.

Preparing time 10 minutes, Total time 10 minutes, Servings: 1

LEMON ORZO

**Nutritional Info: Calories: 191cal, Total fat: 6g, Saturated fat: 1g
Protein: 7g, Carbs: 41.3g, Sodium: 225mg, Fiber: 7g, Sugar: 0g**

Ingredients

- ¼ cup uncooked whole wheat orzo pasta
- 1 tsp. olive oil
- 1 tbsp. grated Parmesan cheese
- ½ tbsp. freshly chopped parsley
- Pinch of grated lemon zest
- Salt and ground black pepper

Instructions

1. Cook orzo as per the packet steps; drain and set aside. Transfer the leftover ingredients to the bowl, drizzle olive oil, and orzo pasta.
2. Mix them well. Serve and enjoy.

Preparing time 10 minutes, Total time 20 minutes, Servings: 1

Diabetes Cookbook

CREAMY AND CHEESY CHICKPEA SALAD

**Nutritional Info: Calories: 81cal, Total fat: 2g, Saturated fat: 0.7g
Protein: 4.9g, Carbs: 18g, Sodium: 235mg, Fiber: 2.5g, Sugar: 3g**

Ingredients

- 3 tbsp. canned chickpeas, rinsed
- ½ cup cucumber, peeled and diced
- 1/3 cup halved cherry tomatoes
- 1 tbsp. crumbled low-fat cottage cheese
- 1 tbsp. diced onion
- 1½ tbsp. creamy dill ranch dressing
- Ground black pepper to taste

Instructions

1. Add chickpeas, diced cucumber, tomatoes, cheese, and onion to a medium bowl.
2. Add dressing and pepper and toss to coat. Serve and enjoy.

Preparing time 10 minutes, Total time 10 minutes, Servings 1

TOMATO, ONION & CUCUMBER SALAD

**Nutritional Info: Calories: 98cal, Total fat: 2.7g, Saturated fat: 0.2g
Protein: 1.6g, Carbs: 16.8g, Sodium: 204mg, Fiber: 2g, Sugar: 6.8g**

Ingredients

- ½ tbsp. rice vinegar
- ½ tsp. canola oil
- 1 tsp. agave nectar
- Salt and ground black pepper to taste
- 1 small cucumber, peeled and sliced
- 1 medium tomato, wedged
- ½ small, sweet onion, roundly sliced
- ½ tbsp. coarsely chopped fresh herbs

Instructions

1. Add vinegar, oil, agave nectar, salt, and pepper to a deep bowl. Remove the peel from the cucumbers in alternating stripes. Sliced cucumbers into thin rounds.
2. Toss in the cucumber slices, tomatoes, and onion with the dressing until everything is well combined. Set aside 30 minutes to an hour. Add the herbs just before serving and toss once more.

Preparing time 10 minutes, Total time 10 minutes, Servings 1

Diabetes Cookbook

EASY CABBAGE SLAW

Nutritional Info: Calories: 96cal, Total fat: 7.5g, Saturated fat: 1g Protein: 2g, Carbs: 5.2g, Sodium: 153mg, Fiber: 1.4g, Sugar: 2.3g

Ingredients

- ½ cup finely shredded green cabbage
- 20g thinly sliced red bell pepper
- 20g thinly sliced red onion
- ½ tbsp. seasoned rice vinegar
- ½ tbsp. extra-virgin olive oil
- Salt and ground black pepper

Instructions

1. Add cabbage, sliced bell pepper, onion slices, vinegar, and oil to a large bowl.
2. Stir in salt and pepper; toss again to combine. Serve and enjoy.

Preparing time 10 minutes, Total time 10 minutes, Servings: 1

SPINACH, WALNUTS & STRAWBERRY SALAD

Nutritional Info: Calories: 156cal, Total fat: 10.7g, Saturated fat: 3.4g Protein: 3g, Carbs: 12g, Sodium: 54mg, Fiber: 1.9g, Sugar: 2.3g

Ingredients

- ¾ tbsp. low-fat cream cheese
- 1 tsp. apple cider vinegar
- ¼ tbsp. extra-virgin olive oil
- 2 tsp. chopped walnuts
- Salt and ground black pepper to taste
- 1¼ oz. packed baby spinach
- ¼ cup sliced strawberries
- ½ tsp. monk fruit sweetener

Instructions

1. Add cream cheese, vinegar, oil, sweetener, salt, and pepper to a large bowl.
2. Add spinach and strawberries with walnuts toss to coat. Serve and enjoy.

Preparing time 10 minutes, Total time 10 minutes, Servings: 1

Diabetes Cookbook

SPINACH AVOCADO SMOOTHIE

Nutritional Info: Calories: 218cal, Total fat: 8g, Saturated fat: 0.1g Protein: 2.5g, Carbs: 19g, Sodium: 6mg, Fiber: 6g, Sugar: 25g

Ingredients

- 1 cup chopped baby spinach
- ½ cup chopped baby kale
- 1 mint sprigs
- ½ avocado, peeled, stoned, and sliced
- ½ tbsp. lemon juice
- 1 cup water
- ¼ cup ice cubes

Instructions

1. In the high-power blender, add all ingredients to it. Blend them well until all the elements turn into smooth form.
2. Transfer it to the serving jar/glass. Serve and enjoy.

Preparing time 10 minutes, Total time 10 minutes, Servings: 1

GRILL CORN

Nutritional Info: Calories: 186cal, Total fat: 6g, Saturated fat: 3g Protein: 5g, Carbs: 28g, Sodium: 180mg, Fiber: 2g, Sugar: 7g

Ingredients

- 1 medium ear of sweet corn
- 1 tbsp. low-fat sour cream
- ¾ tbsp. grated parmesan cheese
- ¾ tsp. lime juice
- Pinch of chili powder
- Pinch of salt and black pepper

Instructions

1. Peel the corn husks within 1 inch of the bottoms and remove the silk. Replace the husks on the corn and secure with kitchen string. Soaked in water for 20 mins. Then cover and grill corn for 20-25 minutes, or until tender, over medium heat, turning frequently.
2. Mix the leftover ingredients in a small bowl until well combined. Remove the string from the corn and peel back the husks. Spread the sour cream mixture over the corn. Serve and enjoy.

Preparing time 10 minutes, Total time 30 minutes, Servings: 1

Diabetes Cookbook

ZUCCHINI PANCAKES

**Nutritional Info: Calories: 186cal, Total fat: 6g, Saturated fat: 3g
Protein: 5g, Carbs: 28g, Sodium: 180mg, Fiber: 2g, Sugar: 7g**

Ingredients

- ¾ cup shredded zucchini
- 1 large egg white
- ½ tbsp. minced garlic
- Salt and pepper to taste
- Pinch of dried oregano
- 2 tbsp. all-purpose flour
- 2 tbsp. finely chopped sweet onion
- ¾ tsp. butter

Instructions

1. Add egg white, garlic, salt, pepper, and oregano to a large bowl, and mix until well combined. Stir in the flour until it is just moistened. Combine zucchini and onion.
2. Grease a skillet lightly with butter and heat over medium heat. Drop 1/4 cupsful of the zucchini mixture onto the skillet; flatten to 12-inch thickness (3-inch diameter). Cook for 4-5 minutes on each side until golden brown. Serve with marinara sauce if desired.

Preparing time 10 minutes, Total time 30 minutes, Servings: 1

EASY POTATO SALAD

**Nutritional Info: Calories: 128cal, Total fat: 3g, Saturated fat: 2g
Protein: 4g, Carbs: 18.5g, Sodium: 190mg, Fiber: 2g, Sugar: 3g**

Ingredients

- 100g small red potatoes, halved
- 3 tbsp. chill tzatziki sauce
- 1 tsp. celery ribs, thinly sliced
- 1 tbsp. low-fat plain Greek yogurt
- 2 tsp. chopped green onions
- ½ tsp. snipped fresh dill
- ½ tsp. minced fresh parsley
- Salt and pepper to taste

Instructions

1. In a Dutch oven, place the potatoes with enough water to cover them. Bring the water to a boil. Uncover, decrease the stove heat to low, and cook for 10-15 minutes, or until vegetables are tender. Drain and allow to cool completely.
2. Add tzatziki sauce, celery, yogurt, green onions, dill, parsley, celery salt, pepper, and, if desired, mint to a small bowl, and mix well. Toss potatoes in the sauce to coat. Refrigerate until cold and covered.

Preparing time 10 minutes, Total time 15 minutes, Servings: 1

Diabetes Cookbook

SESAME GREEN BEANS

**Nutritional Info: Calories: 115cal, Total fat: 3g, Saturated fat: 0g
Protein: 3g, Carbs: 19g, Sodium: 305mg, Fiber: 4g, Sugar: 3g**

Ingredients

- ½ lb. fresh green beans, trimmed
- ¼ tsp. sesame oil
- ¼ tsp. canola oil
- ¼ shallot, finely chopped
- ¼ tbsp. minced garlic
- Salt and pepper to taste
- ½ tsp. sesame seeds, toasted

Instructions

1. Bring 2 1/2-3 cups of water to a boil in a Dutch oven. Cook for 6-8 minutes or until green beans is tender. Meanwhile, add oils to a small skillet, and put it over medium heat.
2. Cook and stir for 2-3 minutes until shallot, garlic, salt, and pepper are tender. Return the green beans to the Dutch oven after draining. Toss in the shallot mixture to coat. Sprinkle sesame seeds on top.

Preparing time 10 minutes, Total time 20 minutes, Servings 1

CORN AND BLACK BEAN SALAD

**Nutritional Info: Calories: 110cal, Total fat: 4g, Saturated fat: 0.5g
Protein: 4g, Carbs: 28.6g, Sodium: 50mg, Fiber: 4g, Sugar: 2g**

Ingredients

- 1¼ oz. canned black beans without liquid
- 30g frozen corn, thawed
- 2 tbsp. diced red bell pepper
- 1 tbsp. diced red onion
- 1 tbsp. chopped fresh cilantro
- 1 tsp. lime juice
- 1 tsp. olive oil
- Salt and black pepper to taste

Instructions

1. Add beans, corn, red pepper, diced red onion, and cilantro to a bowl.
2. In the other bowl, mix the leftover ingredients and pour over bean salad. Toss to coat.

Preparing time 10 minutes, Total time 25 minutes, Servings 1

Diabetes Cookbook

ROASTED BRUSSELS SPROUTS WITH PUMPKIN

Nutritional Info: Calories: 200cal, Total fat: 9g, Saturated fat: 1g
Protein: 4g, Carbs: 25.7g, Sodium: 255mg, Fiber: 3g, Sugar: 4g

Ingredients

- ½ small pie pumpkin (about ½ lb.), peeled and cubed
- 100g fresh Brussels sprouts, trimmed and halved
- ¾ tsp. minced garlic
- 2 tsp. olive oil
- ¼ tbsp. balsamic vinegar
- Salt and coarsely ground pepper
- ¼ tbsp. minced fresh parsley

Instructions

1. Preheat the oven to 400. Add pumpkin, Brussels sprouts, and garlic to a large bowl. Mix oil, vinegar, salt, and pepper in the other small bowl; drizzle over the vegetables and toss to coat.
2. Place in the greased 15x10x1-inch baking pan. Roast for 35-40 minutes, stirring once, or until tender. Serve with a parsley garnish.

Preparing time 15 minutes, Total time 35 minutes, Servings: 1

MANGO CHICKEN SALAD

Nutritional Info: Calories: 210cal, Total fat: 2g, Saturated fat: 0g
Protein: 30g, Carbs: 30g, Sodium: 447mg, Fiber: 4g, Sugar: 16g

Ingredients

- 115g chicken tenderloins
- Salt and black pepper
- 3/2 cup torn mixed salad greens
- 1 tbsp. balsamic vinaigrette
- 1 small mango, peeled and cubed
- ¼ cup fresh snap peas, without sugar, halved lengthwise

Instructions

1. Sprinkle salt and pepper over the chicken. Cover, and grill chicken, on a lightly oiled rack over medium heat until no longer pink, 3-4 minutes on each side.
2. Dice the chicken. Distribute the greens among the plates and drizzle with vinaigrette. Serve immediately with chicken, mango, and peas on top.

Preparing time 10 minutes, Total time 20 minutes, Servings: 1

Diabetes Cookbook

ROASTED CAULIFLOWER RICE

Nutritional Info: Calories: 112cal, **Total fat:** 9g, **Saturated fat:** 4g
Protein: 4g, **Carbs:** 6.5g, **Sodium:** 103mg, **Fiber:** 2g, **Sugar:** 2g

Ingredients

- ½ small head cauliflower
- 1 tsp. unsalted butter
- ½ tsp. extra-virgin olive oil
- ¾ tsp. garlic-herb seasoning blend
- 2 tbsp. finely grated Asiago cheese

Instructions

1. Finely shred cauliflower with a food blender. Add butter, oil, and seasoning blend to large cast iron and put it over medium-high heat.
2. Add the cauliflower when the butter has melted, and stir to combine. Uncover; Cook for 10-15 minutes, or until tender, stirring occasionally. Add the cheese and mix well.

Preparing time 5 minutes, Total time 20 minutes, Servings: 1

TUNA & WHITE BEAN SALAD

Nutritional Info: Calories: 223cal, **Total fat:** 7.5g, **Saturated fat:** 1.1g
Protein: 17g, **Carbs:** 17g, **Sodium:** 532mg, **Fiber:** 6.6g, **Sugar:** 2.8g

Ingredients

- ¾ tbsp. lemon juice
- ¼ tbsp. extra-virgin olive oil
- 1 tsp. minced garlic
- Salt and ground pepper to taste
- 4 oz. canned white kidney beans, rinsed
- 1 tbsp. chopped onion
- ¾ tbsp. chopped fresh parsley
- ¾ tbsp. chopped fresh basil
- 1¼ oz. canned tuna in water drained and flaked

Instructions

1. Add lemon juice, oil, garlic, salt, and pepper to a bowl. Add beans, tuna, onion, chopped parsley, and basil; toss to coat well.

Preparing time 10 minutes, Total time 10 minutes, Servings:

Diabetes Cookbook

SAUTÉED GARLIC GREEN BEANS

**Nutritional Info: Calories: 76cal, Total fat: 3g, Saturated fat: 0g
Protein: 2g, Carbs: 10.7g, Sodium: 85mg, Fiber: 3g, Sugar: 3g**

Ingredients

- ¾ tsp. oil from sun-dried oily tomatoes
- 2 tbsp. sliced sweet onion
- 2 tbsp. chopped oil-packed sun-dried tomatoes
- 1 tsp. minced garlic
- ¼ tsp. lemon-pepper seasoning
- 1½ oz. frozen green beans

Instructions

1. Add oil to the Dutch oven and put it over medium heat. Stir in onion and cook and stir for 3-4 minutes, or until tender. Add tomatoes, garlic, and lemon pepper, and cook for two minutes.
2. Stir in beans, cover, and cook for 7-9 mins. Uncover and cook more for another 2-3 minutes, or until liquid has almost completely evaporated.

Preparing time 10 minutes, Total time 25 minutes, Servings: 1

CORN CARROT EDAMAME SALAD

**Nutritional Info: Calories: 129cal, Total fat: 5g, Saturated fat: 0g
Protein: 6g, Carbs: 14.4g, Sodium: 533mg, Fiber: 3.2g, Sugar: 4.3g**

Ingredients

- ¼ cup frozen shelled edamame
- ¼ cup julienned carrots
- ¼ cup frozen corn, thawed
- 1 tbsp. chopped green onions
- ¼ tbsp. minced fresh cilantro
- 2 tbsp. salad vinaigrette
- ¼ cup sliced mushrooms

Instructions

1. In a small saucepan, add edamame with mushrooms; add enough water to cover. Boil the water, then reduce to low heat and cook for 4-5 minutes, or until the vegetables are tender.
2. Drain and cool slightly in a large mixing bowl. Stir in carrots, corn, green onions, and cilantro. Toss the salad with the vinaigrette. Cover and chill for at least 2 hours before serving.

Preparing time 10 minutes, Total time: 25 minutes, Servings: 1

EASY CUCUMBER KIMCHI

**Nutritional Info: Calories: 10cal, Total fat: 0.1g, Saturated fat: 0g
Protein: 0.3g, Carbs: 7g, Sodium: 64mg, Fiber: 0.3g, Sugar: 0.5g**

Ingredients

- 1 small cucumber (about 1½ ounces), halved and lengthy dice
- Salt to taste
- 1 tsp. chopped garlic
- 1 tbsp. chopped scallions, only white and light green parts
- ½-inch fresh ginger, peeled and chopped
- 1 tsp. rice vinegar
- ½ tsp. chili powder
- ¼ tsp. monk fruit sweetener
- ¼ tsp. fish sauce

Instructions

1. In a bowl, add cucumber with salt and toss well. Set aside 30 minutes. Add garlic, scallions, ginger, vinegar, chili powder, monk fruit, and fish sauce to the other bowl.
2. Remove the cucumbers from the water. Place the cucumbers into the vinegar mixture. Before serving, cover and chill for 8-12 hours.

Preparing time 10 minutes, Total time 40 minutes, Servings 1

BELL PEPPER QUINOA SALAD

**Nutritional Info: Calories: 129cal, Total fat: 5g, Saturated fat: 0g
Protein: 6g, Carbs: 15g, Sodium: 533mg, Fiber: 3.2g, Sugar: 4.3g**

Ingredients

- ¼ cup water
- 1 tbsp. quinoa, rinsed
- ¼ cup freshly sliced baby spinach
- 2 cherry tomatoes, halved
- 1 small cucumber, seedless and chopped
- ½ small orange bell pepper, chopped
- ½ small yellow bell pepper, chopped
- 1 tbsp. chopped green onions
- 2 tbsp. sweet and spicy lemon dressing (zero sugar)

Instructions

1. In a large saucepan, bring water to a boil. Add quinoa. Reduce heat; simmer, covered until liquid is absorbed, 12-15 minutes. Remove from heat, and fluff with a fork. Transfer to a large bowl; cool completely.
2. Stir spinach, tomatoes, cucumber, peppers, and green onions into quinoa. Drizzle lemon dressing over quinoa mixture; toss to coat. Refrigerate until serving.

Preparing time 10 minutes, Total time 25 minutes, Servings 1

Diabetes Cookbook

AIR FRIED BEETS WITH COTTAGE CHEESE

**Nutritional Info: Calories: 122cal, Total fat: 6g, Saturated fat: 2g
Protein: 3g, Carbs: 14g, Sodium: 320mg, Fiber: 3g, Sugar: 8g**

Ingredients

- 1 small beet, trimmed, peeled, and cubed
- ¾ tsp. extra-virgin olive oil
- Salt and ground black pepper
- 20g low-fat cottage cheese cubes
- 1 tsp. fresh chopped oregano

Instructions

1. Heat your air fryer to 400 for 5 minutes. Add beets to the large bowl with the oil, salt, and black pepper, and toss to coat.
2. In the fryer basket, arrange the beets in a single layer and cook for 10 minutes. Cook until the beets are crispy and browned around the edges, about 6 to 8 minutes.
3. Top with feta and oregano and transfer to a serving dish.

Preparing time 10 minutes, Total time 30 minutes, Servings: 1

KIDNEY BEANS AND BROWN RICE SALAD

**Nutritional Info: Calories: 307cal, Total fat: 8.4g, Saturated fat: 1.1g
Protein: 11g, Carbs: 43g, Sodium: 63mg, Fiber: 7.5g, Sugar: 1.9g**

Ingredients

- ½ cup brown rice
- ½ cup red kidney beans, drain and wash
- 4½ tsp. vegetable stock
- ¾ tsp. minced garlic cloves
- 2 tbsp. chopped onions
- ½ tbsp. grapeseed oil
- Salt and freshly ground peppers
- 1 tbsp. chopped thyme

Instructions

1. Prepare rice as per the packet steps. Fry the onion rings in the oil until golden brown. Add the garlic and beans, cook for a few minutes, then add the stock.
2. Remove the thyme leaves from their stalks and combine them with the beans and onions in the cooked rice. Sprinkle salt and pepper to taste, and garnish with thyme.

Preparing time 10 minutes, Total time 25 minutes, Servings: 1

LEMON BROCCOLI COUSCOUS

**Nutritional Info: Calories: 155cal, Total fat: 3g, Saturated fat: 0g
Protein: 5g, Carbs: 27g, Sodium: 328mg, Fiber: 4g, Sugar: 1g**

Ingredients

- ½ tsp. olive oil
- 2/3 cup fresh broccoli florets, chopped
- 28g uncooked whole-wheat couscous
- ½ tsp. minced garlic
- 3½ tbsp. reduced-sodium chicken broth
- Pinch of grated lemon zest
- ¼ tsp. lemon juice
- Salt and black pepper to taste
- Pinch of dried basil
- ½ tsp. slivered almonds, toasted

Instructions

1. Add oil to the large cast-iron skillet and put it over medium-high heat. Cook, frequently stirring, until the broccoli is crisp-tender. Stir, and cook more for 1-2 minutes after adding the couscous and garlic.
2. Add broth, lemon zest, lemon juice, seasonings, and boil. Remove from the heat; cover, set aside, for 5-10 minutes until the broth has been absorbed. Using a fork, fluff the mixture. Sprinkle almonds on top.

Preparing time 10 minutes, Total time 25 minutes, Servings: 1

SPINACH BLACKBERRY SALAD

**Nutritional Info: Calories: 106cal, Total fat: 7g, Saturated fat: 1g
Protein: 3g, Carbs: 10.2g, Sodium: 230mg, Fiber: 4g, Sugar: 4g**

Ingredients

- ½ cup fresh baby spinach
- 1/3 cup fresh blackberries, halved
- ¼ cup cherry tomatoes halved
- 1 tbsp. crumbled low-fat cottage cheese
- 1 tsp. balsamic vinaigrette

Instructions

1. Add tomatoes, spinach, and top with berry and crumble cottage cheese in a large bowl.
2. Toss them well until combined. Serve and enjoy.

Preparing time 10 minutes, Total time 10 minutes, Servings: 1

Diabetes Cookbook

MEAT

MEAT SAUCE WITH SPAGHETTI

**Nutritional Info: Calories: 352cal, Total fat: 23.5g, Saturated fat: 8g
Protein: 12g, Carbs: 23g, Sodium: 240mg, Fiber: 3.6g, Sugar: 3.6g**

Ingredients

- 60g whole-wheat fresh spaghetti
- ¼ tsp. extra-virgin olive oil
- 2 tbsp. chopped onion
- 2 tbsp. chopped carrot
- 1 tbsp. chopped celery
- 1 tsp. minced garlic
- 1 tsp. Italian seasoning
- 60g lean ground beef
- 3 oz. canned crushed tomatoes
- ½ tbsp. chopped flat-leaf parsley
- Salt to taste

Instructions

1. Boil pasta as per instructions until just tender. Drain. In the meantime, heat oil in a skillet on medium. Add onion, carrot, celery and cook for about 7 minutes until the onion has softened.
2. Stir in beef, seasoning, and garlic. Cook for 5 minutes. Raise the heat. Add salt and tomatoes; cook for 6 minutes until thickened. Enjoy the pasta and sauce together.

Preparing time 10 minutes, Total time 30 minutes, Servings: 1

AIR-FRYER BEEF MEATBALLS

**Nutritional Info: Calories: 461cal, Total fat: 36g, Saturated fat: 14g
Protein: 20.4g, Carbs: 14.7g, Sodium: 192mg, Fiber: 1.7g, Sugar: 0.6g**

Ingredients

- 115g lean ground beef
- 2 tbsp. chopped onion
- ½ tbsp. grated Parmesan cheese
- ¾ tbsp. whole-wheat panko breadcrumbs
- 1 small egg, lightly beaten
- ¼ tsp. Italian seasoning
- Salt and pepper to taste
- 1/8 tsp. garlic powder
- 1/8 tsp. onion powder

Instructions

1. Preheat the air fryer to 370°F. Grease the basket for the air fryer. Add beef, onion, Parmesan, panko, egg, Italian seasoning, salt, garlic, and onion powder with pepper in a bowl. Shape the beef mixture into meatballs.
2. Put meatballs in the fryer basket in a single layer. Spray cooking spray on the meatballs' tops. Cook for 8 minutes or until the top is just beginning to brown. If desired, serve with tomato sauce.

Preparing time 10 minutes, Total time 35 minutes, Servings: 1

Diabetes Cookbook

GRILLED VEGGIE BEEF KEBABS

**Nutritional Info: Calories: 237cal, Total fat: 20g, Saturated fat: 2g
Protein: 25g, Carbs: 14g, Sodium: 95mg, Fiber: 1.7g, Sugar: 0.6g**

Ingredients

- 3 tbsp. sugar free balsamic vinegar
- 1 tbsp. extra-virgin olive oil
- ½ tbsp. whole-grain mustard
- ¼ tbsp. dried oregano
- ¼ tbsp. dried rosemary
- 1 tsp. minced garlic
- Salt and ground pepper to taste
- 115g tri-tip sirloin steak, trimmed and cubed
- 4 button mushrooms
- 4 cherry tomatoes
- ½ small bell pepper
- 4 1-inch chunks of red onion

Instructions

1. Add oil, mustard, oregano, rosemary, garlic, salt, and pepper on two skewers, thread beef, mushrooms, tomatoes, bell pepper chunks, and onions in a small bowl. In a baking dish, place the kebabs and marinate for at least two hours.
2. Set the grill heat to medium-high heat. Grill the kebabs for 8 minutes. Hold the skewers over the flames for about 15 minutes, turning them frequently, to grill over your campfire.

Preparing time 10 minutes, Total time 35 minutes, Servings: 1

EASY MEATLOAF

**Nutritional Info: Calories: 332cal, Total fat: 20g, Saturated fat: 6g
Protein: 28g, Carbs: 10g, Sodium: 515mg, Fiber: 5g, Sugar: 4.6g**

Ingredients

- 100g ground beef
- 1 tbsp. diced onion
- 1½ tsp. minced garlic
- 1 tbsp. flax seed meal
- 1 small egg
- ¾ tsp. Worcestershire sauce
- 1 tbsp. tomato paste
- ¼ tsp. dried oregano
- Salt and pepper to taste

Instructions

1. Grease a loaf pan and set your oven to 350 degrees F. Sauté onion with garlic in a pan over medium heat for 2 minutes. Add ground beef, flax seed meal, eggs, sauce, tomato paste, dried oregano, salt, and pepper to the other bowl, along with the onion and garlic.
2. Mix well. Place the meatloaf in the loaf pan and bake for 60 minutes, or until thoroughly cooked. Slice and serve with sauce after cooling.

Preparing time 10 minutes, Total time 80 minutes, Servings: 1

Diabetes Cookbook

STUFFED BELL PEPPERS

Nutritional Info: Calories: 257cal, Total fat: 9g, Saturated fat: 3g Protein: 17g, Carbs: 27g, Sodium: 650mg, Fiber: 4g, Sugar: 8g

Ingredients

- 1 large green pepper, scoop out inner of bell pepper
- 50g lean ground beef
- 1 tbsp. chopped onion
- ¼ cup canned whole tomatoes
- ¼ cup cooked brown rice
- ¼ tbsp. Worcestershire sauce
- 1/8 tsp. Italian seasoning
- ¼ cup tomato sauce

Instructions

1. Boil the water, add pepper; cook for 8 minutes; drain. Cook meat and onion in a skillet over medium heat. Cook tomatoes until liquid evaporates. After taking the meat mixture off the heat, add the rice, sauce, and seasoning.
2. Spoon mixture into pepper in portions of 1/2 cup. Bake for 20 minutes at 350°F, or until just lightly browned. After topping the peppers with tomato sauce, reheat the oven.

Preparing time 10 minutes, Total time 80 minutes, Servings 1

BEEF CASSEROLE STEW

Nutritional Info: Calories: 176cal, Total fat: 4g, Saturated fat: 2g Protein: 15g, Carbs: 20g, Sodium: 80mg, Fiber: 2g, Sugar: 1g

Ingredients

- 60g beef meat, cubed
- 80g quartered potatoes
- 1 oz. sliced fresh mushrooms
- 2 small baby carrots, halved
- Salt and black pepper to taste
- Pinch of dried thyme
- ½ tsp. flour
- 1 oz. fat-free reduced-sodium beef broth

Instructions

1. Coat the microwave-safe baking dish lightly. Add potatoes, mushrooms, and carrots with the beef. Combine flour, thyme, salt, and pepper in a small bowl. Sprinkle over the stew mixture evenly.
2. Over the meat and vegetables, pour the broth. Cover the dish with waxed pepper. Microwave on high for 30 minutes. Remove the dish; set aside for five minutes before serving.

Preparing time 10 minutes, Total time 45 minutes, Servings 1

Diabetes Cookbook

ZUCCHINI BOATS

**Nutritional Info: Calories: 316cal, Total fat: 16g, Saturated fat: 6g
Protein: 32g, Carbs: 15g, Sodium: 714mg, Fiber: 7g, Sugar: 9g**

Ingredients

- 1 medium zucchini, lengthily halved, scoop out flesh
- 100g lean ground beef
- 2 tbsp. chopped onion
- 1 tbsp. chopped sweet red pepper
- ¼ cup tomato sauce
- 2 tbsp. bulgur
- Salt and pepper to taste
- 2 tbsp. tomato salsa
- 2 tbsp. shredded low-fat cheddar cheese

Instructions

1. Set the oven temperature to 350°F to preheat. Add beef, onion, and red pepper to a skillet; cook over medium heat for 8 minutes or until the meat is done. Add bulgur, pepper, tomato sauce, and zucchini flesh to the mixture, up to a boil.
2. Simmer for 12–15 minutes at reduced heat. Mix in salsa. Mixture into zucchini boats with a spoon. Place in the baking dish and cook for 20 minutes, covered. Sprinkle cheese on top and bake the zucchini uncovered for 15 minutes.

Preparing time 10 minutes, Total time 45 minutes, Servings 1

SAUTÉED GROUND BEEF AND BEANS

**Nutritional Info: Calories: 286cal, Total fat: 10g, Saturated fat: 5g
Protein: 23g, Carbs: 26g, Sodium: 525mg, Fiber: 7g, Sugar: 7g**

Ingredients

- ½ tsp. extra-virgin olive oil
- 2 tbsp. chopped onion
- 75g ground beef
- 2½ oz. canned no-salt-added navy beans, rinsed
- 3 tbsp. water
- 2½ tbsp. ketchup
- 1 tsp. agave nectar
- 1/8 tsp. Dijon mustard
- Salt and pepper to taste

Instructions

1. In a saucepan, add oil, and put it over medium-high heat. Add ground beef with onion. Cook for 5 minutes until the beef is no longer pink and the onion softened.
2. Bring the beans, water, ketchup, molasses, mustard, and salt to a simmer. Reduce heat and continue cooking for 5-8 minutes until the mixture bubbles and thickens. Serve and garnish as desired.

Preparing time 10 minutes, Total time 25 minutes, Servings 1

Diabetes Cookbook

BEEF STROGANOFF

**Nutritional Info: Calories: 249cal, Total fat: 7g, Saturated fat: 2.5g
Protein: 23g, Carbs: 23.5g, Sodium: 250mg, Fiber: 4g, Sugar: 3g**

Ingredients

- 1 oz. whole grain fresh egg noodles
- ¼ tsp. olive oil
- 90 beef tenderloin
- ¼ cup sliced white mushrooms
- 1 tbsp. chopped onion
- ¾ tsp. all-purpose flour
- 1 tbsp. dry white wine
- ¼ tsp. Dijon Mustard
- 1 oz. fat free, low sodium beef broth
- 1½ tbsp. fat-free sour cream
- Salt and pepper to taste

Instructions

1. Prepare noodles as directed on the packet. Over high heat, put a pan with oil, add the meat, and cook for about 3 minutes. Remove meat and add onion and mushrooms and sauté for five mins.
2. Cook for 3 minutes after adding flour and dry wine. Boil after adding beef broth and Dijon mustard. Decrease the stove heat to low, then simmer for five minutes. Simmer the beef, sour cream, salt, and pepper for three minutes. Over whole-grain egg noodles, serve.

Preparing time 5 minutes, Total time 15 minutes, Servings 1

BEEF STIR-FRY

**Nutritional Info: Calories: 203cal, Total fat: 3g, Saturated fat: 1g
Protein: 26g, Carbs: 18g, Sodium: 283mg, Fiber: 1g, Sugar: 1g**

Ingredients

- 3 oz. beef tenderloin, cubed
- 4 oz. frozen, mixed vegetables, thawed
- ¾ tbsp. lite low-sodium teriyaki sauce

Instructions

1. Add meat to the nonstick pan and cook for 5 minutes until browned. Raise the heat. Stir in vegetables and teriyaki sauce.
2. Cook for 6 minutes or until the meat is thoroughly heated and the vegetables are crisp-tender. Serve with baked potatoes, brown rice, pasta, or alone.

Preparing time 5 minutes, Total time 20 minutes, Servings 1

Diabetes Cookbook

GRILL BEEF BURGERS

Nutritional Info: Calories: 181cal, **Total fat:** 9g, **Saturated fat:** 4g
Protein: 22g, **Carbs:** 3g, **Sodium:** 260mg, **Fiber:** 1g, **Sugar:** 2g

Ingredients

- 35g chopped onion
- ½ tbsp. chopped fresh parsley
- ½ tbsp. chopped fresh mint
- ¼ tsp. ground garlic
- 1/8 tsp. ground allspice
- 1/8 tsp. pepper
- Pinch of ground cinnamon
- Salt and pepper to taste
- 100g lean ground beef

Instructions

1. Mix each ingredient (except beef). Add beef and stir just enough to combine. Shape patties as desired.
2. Cover and grill patties over medium heat for 4-6 minutes per side. Serve with sauce and, if desired, place on lettuce leaves.

Preparing time 5 minutes, Total time 20 minutes, Servings 1

AIR-FRYER LAMB CHOPS

Nutritional Info: Calories: 133cal, **Total fat:** 7g, **Saturated fat:** 2g
Protein: 16g, **Carbs:** 2g, **Sodium:** 336mg, **Fiber:** 1g, **Sugar:** 0g

Ingredients

- 1 tbsp. extra-virgin olive oil
- ½ tbsp. red-wine vinegar
- ¼ tbsp. chopped fresh rosemary
- ½ tsp. chopped fresh oregano
- ¼ tsp. grated lemon zest
- 1 tsp. minced garlic
- Salt and black pepper
- 2 lamb chops

Instructions

1. Add oil, vinegar, rosemary, oregano, lemon zest, salt, and pepper to a bowl, and mix well; now add lamb chops. Give it 20 minutes to marinate.
2. Preheat the air fryer to 380°F. Lightly grease the basket, then lay the chops in a single layer in the air fryer basket. Cook for 4 minutes or until the chops start too lightly brown. Flip; cook for 4 to 5 minutes.

Preparing time 5 minutes, Total time 20 minutes, Servings 1

Diabetes Cookbook

GLAZED PORK CHOPS

Nutritional Info: Calories: 403cal, **Total fat:** 26.5g, **Saturated fat:** 6g
Protein: 25g, **Carbs:** 16g, **Sodium:** 353mg, **Fiber:** 2g, **Sugar:** 14g

Ingredients

- 1 pork loin chop, thin cut (100g weight)
- ¼ tsp. minced fresh thyme
- Salt and pepper to taste
- ¼ tbsp. olive oil
- 2 tbsp. brewed coffee
- 1 tbsp. agave nectar
- ¾ tsp. Dijon mustard
- ¼ tsp. Worcestershire sauce

Instructions

1. Rub salt, pepper, and thyme into the pork chops. In a skillet, sauté the pork chops. Remove and keep warm. To the skillet, add the leftover ingredients. Boil until the liquid is cut in half.
2. Put the pork chops back in the skillet. Reduce heat, cover, and simmer the meat for 10 to 12 minutes, turning it once until it is tender. Take with sauce.

Preparing time 5 minutes, Total time 20 minutes, Servings 1

GRILLED PORK WITH PINEAPPLE

Nutritional Info: Calories: 299cal, **Total fat:** 14.5g, **Saturated fat:** 4.5g
Protein: 26g, **Carbs:** 16g, **Sodium:** 451mg, **Fiber:** 1.8g, **Sugar:** 7.5g

Ingredients

- 4 oz. pork tenderloins
- ½ tbsp. soy sauce
- ½ tbsp. minced garlic
- ½ tbsp. minced ginger
- Salt and black pepper to taste
- 1 fresh pineapple chuck

Instructions

1. Mix the marinade ingredients in a tight, sealed plastic bag, then add pork. Marinate for 2 –to overnight. Turn on a grill, cover it, and cook each side for about 10 minutes.
2. Place the pineapple chunks on the grill, turning every three minutes for the final six minutes of grilling. Slice the pork and pineapple before serving.

Preparing time 5 minutes, Total time 20 minutes, Servings 1

Diabetes Cookbook

GRILLED BEEF CHIMICHANGAS

**Nutritional Info: Calories: 315cal, Total fat: 12g, Saturated fat: 5g
Protein: 22g, Carbs: 30g, Sodium: 370mg, Fiber: 4g, Sugar: 1g**

Ingredients

- 80g lean ground beef
- 2 tbsp. chopped onion
- 1 tsp. minced garlic
- ¾ oz. chopped green chiles
- ¾ tbsp. salsa
- Pinch of ground cumin
- 1 whole wheat tortillas
- 2 tbsp. low fat shredded cottage cheese

Instructions

1. Cook beef with onion and garlic in a skillet for 8 minutes over moderate heat. Add cumin, salsa, and chili. Top the tortilla with cheese and spoon ½ cup of the beef mixture over it.
2. Roll up the tortilla by folding the bottom and sides over the filling. Cook for 12 minutes, turning once, over medium-low heat, until crisp and browned. Serve with guacamole and sour cream, if desired.

Preparing time 5 minutes, Total time 25 minutes, Servings: 1

BEEF STEAK FAJITAS

**Nutritional Info: Calories: 417cal, Total fat: 23g, Saturated fat: 8g
Protein: 33g, Carbs: 19.6g, Sodium: 686mg, Fiber: 5g, Sugar: 6g**

Ingredients

- 125g beef top sirloin steak, thin slices
- ½ tbsp. fajita seasoning mix
- ½ of an onion
- ½ of a sweet red pepper
- ½ of a green pepper
- ¼ tbsp. olive oil

Instructions

1. Rub steak with seasoning spices. Apply oil to the onion and peppers. Over medium-high direct heat, grill the steak and vegetables for 4-6 minutes on each side, covered.
2. Rest for five minutes before slicing. Slice steak and vegetables into strips. Enjoy after serving.

Preparing time 10 minutes, Total time 25 minutes, Servings: 1

Diabetes Cookbook

MARINATED PORK SKEWER

**Nutritional Info: Calories: 343cal, Total fat: 15g, Saturated fat: 5.6g
Protein: 32g, Carbs: 20g, Sodium: 412mg, Fiber: 4g, Sugar: 7g**

Ingredients

- ¼ cup low-fat plain yogurt
- ½ tbsp. lemon juice
- ¼ minced garlic
- Pinch of ground cumin
- Pinch of ground coriander
- 100g pork tenderloin, cubed
- 1 small onion, halved
- 1 cherry tomato
- ½ small sweet red pepper, halved
- ½ small green pepper, halved

Instructions

1. Mix yogurt, lemon juice, garlic, cumin, and coriander in a glass bowl. Add pork, cover, and marinade for six or more hours.
2. On a skewer, thread peppers, tomatoes, onions, and pork. Grill the meat for 35 minutes or until done over medium heat.

Preparing time 5 minutes, Total time 30 minutes, Servings: 1

PORK CHOPS WITH CREAMY MUSHROOM SAUCE

**Nutritional Info: Calories: 324cal, Total fat: 20g, Saturated fat: 5.8g
Protein: 30g, Carbs: 7.5g, Sodium: 362mg, Fiber: 0.9g, Sugar: 2.8g**

Ingredients

- 1 pork chop (115g), thick cut and fat trimmed
- Salt and ground pepper to taste
- ¾ tbsp. extra-virgin olive oil, divided
- 1¼ tbsp. minced shallot
- 2 oz. sliced mushrooms
- 2 tbsp. dry white wine
- 1¼ tbsp. low fat half-and-half cream
- 2 tbsp. chopped herbs

Instructions

1. Rub pork chops as desired with salt and pepper. In a skillet, add 1 tbsp oil, and put it over medium-high heat. Cook the chops for about 7 mins. To the pan, add the leftover oil.
2. Add shallots and mushrooms; cook for 4 minutes or until the mushrooms are browned. Add wine and salt as needed; cook for three minutes or until finished.
3. Add the cream herbs and continue to cook for about one minute. Enjoy after serving.

Preparing time 5 minutes, Total time 20 minutes, Servings: 1

Diabetes Cookbook

LAMB AND VEGGIES STEW

Nutritional Info: Calories: 203cal, Total fat: 4g, Saturated fat: 1g
Protein: 21g, Carbs: 20.7g, Sodium: 182mg, Fiber: 3g, Sugar: 7g

Ingredients

- ½ small red bell pepper, diced
- ½ small carrot, sliced
- ½ small new potato, diced
- 1 tsp. minced garlic
- 2 tbsp. reduced-sodium chicken broth
- 1/8 tsp. dried thyme
- 1/4 teaspoon dried rosemary
- Salt and black pepper to taste
- 3 oz. lamb shoulder meat, cubed
- ½ tbsp. all-purpose flour

Instructions

1. Add garlic, bell pepper, carrot, and potato to the cooker. Stir in the black pepper, rosemary, thyme, and chicken broth. Add lamb and cook for 30 minutes with the lid on high.
2. In a bowl, mix 2 tbsp of water and the flour. Add flour mixture to the cooker. Cover; cook for ten minutes.

Preparing time 5 minutes, Total time 45 minutes, Servings 1

WHITE BEAN AND LAMB STEW

Nutritional Info: Calories: 308cal, Total fat: 7.5g, Saturated fat: 2.8g
Protein: 27g, Carbs: 29g, Sodium: 182mg, Fiber: 16g, Sugar: 13.5g

Ingredients

- 80g very lean lamb, diced
- ¼ cup chopped onion
- 1 tbsp. chopped celery stalks
- ¼ cup chopped carrots
- 1 tsp. sliced garlic
- 1 tsp. Worcestershire sauce
- 100g canned chopped tomatoes, no-sugar added
- 200g canned beans, drained and rinsed
- 300ml water

Instructions

1. Set the oven temperature to 350° F to preheat. Lightly coat the skillet with oil and fry the lamb until browned. Add onion, celery, carrots, garlic, and rosemary to the pan. Cook for 10 mins or until the vegetables are soft.
2. Add bay leaves, tomatoes, Worcestershire sauce, and lamb to the pan. Pour in 300ml of water and stir. Cover 35 mins. Add the beans, stir well, and cook more for 15 mins.

Preparing time 10 minutes, Total time 70 minutes, Servings 1

Diabetes Cookbook

MINCED LAMB AND CHICKPEAS

**Nutritional Info: Calories: 351cal, Total fat: 17g, Saturated fat: 7.6g
Protein: 20g, Carbs: 29.6g, Sodium: 230mg, Fiber: 5.7g, Sugar: 7.5g**

Ingredients

- 75g ground lamb
- 75g canned chickpeas, rinsed
- 2 tbsp. chopped fresh spinach
- ½ cup shredded carrots
- 3 tbsp. chicken broth
- 1 tsp. curry paste
- 1 tsp. turmeric powder
- 1 tsp. lemon juice

Instructions

1. Brown ground lamb and add spices. Add chickpeas, chicken broth, and carrots, and let cook for 5 mins.
2. Add spinach to the pan, top with lemon juice, cover, and let the spinach steam for about 10 mins. Serve and savor with rice or bread.

Preparing time 5 minutes, Total time 35 minutes, Servings: 1

LAMB CURRY

**Nutritional Info: Calories: 274cal, Total fat: 14g, Saturated fat: 6.5g
Protein: 28g, Carbs: 9g, Sodium: 115mg, Fiber: 2.4g, Sugar: 3g**

Ingredients

- 150g leg meat of lamb, cubed into bite size
- ½ large onions, chopped
- ½-inch fresh ginger, sliced
- ½ tbsp. chopped garlic
- 1 green chili, chopped
- 15g chopped tomatoes
- ¾ tsp. garam masala
- ¼ tsp. turmeric powder
- 1 tsp. chili powder
- ½ tbsp. olive oil
- Salt to taste

Instructions

1. Add green chili, onion, ginger, and garlic to the saucepan with olive oil, and cook for two minutes. Add the lamb pieces and continue stirring over high heat until the meat is thoroughly browned.
2. Add tomatoes and cook until amalgamated. Now add salt, turmeric powder, garam masala, and chili powder. Cover; cook for 20 mins. Serve with rice or bread.

Preparing time: 15 minutes, Total time 45 minutes, Servings: 1

Diabetes Cookbook

BROILED LAMB CHOPS

**Nutritional Info: Calories: 182cal, Total fat: 22g, Saturated fat: 2g
Protein: 21g, Carbs: 5.6g, Sodium: 657mg, Fiber: 3.2g, Sugar: 1.8g**

Ingredients

- 4 oz. lamb chops, 1 inch thick
- ½ tsp. oregano
- Salt and black pepper
- 1 lemon, for juice and wedged
- 2 sprigs parsley

Instructions

1. Pour lemon juice, sprinkle salt and pepper on the lamb chop side, then rub oregano. Broil for 8 mins on one side. Then flip and rub salt and pepper.
2. Pour again lemon juice, then again rub oregano on the second side. Broil for 8 mins. Enjoy after serving.

Preparing time 5 minutes, Total time 21 minutes, Servings: 1

BAKED BONELESS PORK CHOPS IN TOMATO SAUCE

**Nutritional Info: Calories: 353cal, Total fat: 17g, Saturated fat: 8g
Protein: 30g, Carbs: 20g, Sodium: 796mg, Fiber: 4.4g, Sugar: 7.5g**

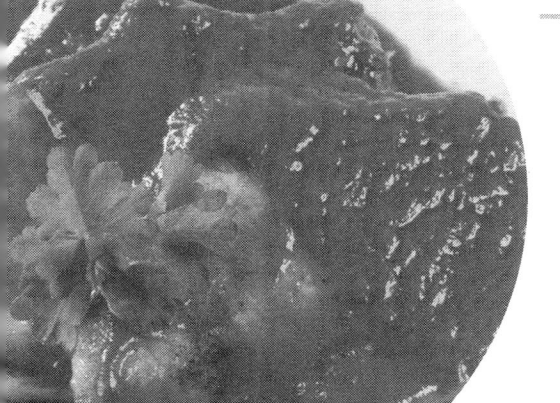

Ingredients

- 1 thick cut pork chop, 100g
- ¼ cup chopped onion
- 1 tsp. minced garlic
- ¾ cup canned tomatoes
- 4 tbsp. chicken broth
- ¼ tsp. paprika powder
- ¼ tsp. dried oregano
- Salt & pepper

Instructions

1. Set the oven heat to 400°F to preheat. Over medium-high heat, put a pan. Sear the pork chops for 2 minutes on each side, then sprinkle pepper on both sides. Remove the chops and put them in the baking dish.
2. Bake for a minute on each side after adding onion and garlic. For two minutes, bake after adding tomato, broth, and spices. Over the pork chops, spoon the tomato sauce. Enjoy after serving.

Preparing time 5 minutes, Total time 15 minutes, Servings: 1

Diabetes Cookbook

PORK CHOP CASSEROLE

Nutritional Info: Calories: 353cal, Total fat: 11g, Saturated fat: 2.7g
Protein: 22g, Carbs: 23g, Sodium: 546mg, Fiber: 1.4g, Sugar: 3.2g

Ingredients

- ¼ tbsp. canola oil
- ¼ cup chopped onion
- 1 tbsp. all-purpose flour
- Salt and black pepper
- 1 pork loin chop
- 2¾ oz. canned condensed cream of mushroom soup
- ¼ tsp. Dijon mustard
- 3 tbsp. low-sodium chicken broth
- ¼ cup sliced mushrooms

Instructions

1. Set the oven heat to 350°F. Grease the baking pan. Add oil to the skillet, and put it over medium-high heat, then add onions, and sauté for 12 minutes. Take out onto a plate.
2. Combine the flour, salt, pepper, and pork in a dish. Cook for 4-5 minutes, or until both sides are browned. Put inside a baking dish. Heat the leftover ingredients for 5 minutes or until hot. Pour over pork chops for 30 mins. Enjoy.

Preparing time 10 minutes, Total time 50 minutes, Servings: 1

AIR FRYER PORK DUMPLINGS

Nutritional Info: Calories: 218cal, Total fat: 10g, Saturated fat: 2.4g
Protein: 15g, Carbs: 17g, Sodium: 817mg, Fiber: 1.6g, Sugar: 0.1g

Ingredients

- 55g ground pork
- 1 tbsp. canned water chestnuts, drained and chopped
- 1 tbsp. canned shiitake mushrooms, drained and chopped
- ¼ sp. soy sauce
- ¼ tsp. sesame oil
- ¼ tsp. sriracha sauce
- 1 serving of round dumpling wrappers (about 4-5)

Instructions

1. Set 400°F temperature on your air fryer. Add meat, water chestnuts, mushrooms, sesame oil, soy sauce, and Sriracha in a skillet, stir and cook over medium heat. Cook for about 6 minutes.
2. Then remove; set aside. Lay out 4 dumpling wrappers, then top each with a heaping teaspoon of the pork mixture. Seal the sides of the wrappers. Cook for 3 minutes in the fryer.

Preparing time 10 minutes, Total time 35 minutes, Servings: 1

Diabetes Cookbook

GRILLED VEGGIE BEEF KEBABS

Nutritional Info: Calories: 237cal, **Total fat:** 20g, **Saturated fat:** 2g
Protein: 25g, **Carbs:** 14g, **Sodium:** 95mg, **Fiber:** 1.7g, **Sugar:** 0.6g

Ingredients

- 3 tbsp. sugar free balsamic vinegar
- 1 tbsp. extra-virgin olive oil
- ½ tbsp. whole-grain mustard
- ¼ tbsp. dried oregano
- ¼ tbsp. dried rosemary
- 1 tsp. minced garlic
- Salt and ground pepper to taste
- 115g tri-tip sirloin steak, trimmed and cubed
- 4 button mushrooms
- 4 cherry tomatoes
- ½ small bell pepper
- 4 1-inch chunks of red onion

Instructions

1. Add oil, mustard, oregano, rosemary, garlic, salt, and pepper on two skewers, thread beef, mushrooms, tomatoes, bell pepper chunks, and onions in a small bowl. In a baking dish, place the kebabs and marinate for at least two hours.
2. Set the grill heat to medium-high heat. Grill the kebabs for 8 minutes. Hold the skewers over the flames for about 15 minutes, turning them frequently, to grill over your campfire.

Preparing time 10 minutes. Total time 35 minutes. Servings: 1

POULTRY

Diabetes Cookbook

TURKEY CHILI

Nutritional Info: Calories: 248cal, **Total fat:** 7.6g, **Saturated fat:** 2.3g
Protein: 25g, **Carbs:** 20g, **Sodium:** 728mg, **Fiber:** 2.4g, **Sugar:** 1.9g

Ingredients

- 4 oz. ground turkey, breast meat
- ¼ of a medium jalapeño
- ½ tsp. chopped red chili
- ½ cup chopped tomatoes
- 1½ tbsp. canned black beans
- ½ tbsp. minced garlic
- 1½ tbsp. onion
- 2 tbsp. chicken stock
- ¼ tsp. paprika powder
- ¼ tbsp. chopped green onion
- 1 tbsp. fat-free sour cream
- Salt and pepper to taste

Instructions

1. Add jalapeno, red chili, onion, and garlic to the pan. Sauté for 4 minutes. Add ground turkey, stir well, and cook more for 5 minutes.
2. Stir in tomatoes, black beans, chicken stock, and spices, and simmer for 15 minutes. Enjoy after serving.

Preparing time 5 minutes, Total time 30 minutes, Servings: 1

TURKEY PATTIES WITH AVOCADO CORN SALSA

Nutritional Info: Calories: 262cal, **Total fat:** 15g, **Saturated fat:** 5g
Protein: 26g, **Carbs:** 5.7g, **Sodium:** 236mg, **Fiber:** 2.7g, **Sugar:** 0.6g

Ingredients

- ½ cup ground turkey, breast meat
- ½ of a medium avocado, half mashed & half diced
- 1 small egg white
- 2 tbsp. canned corn
- ¼ tbsp. minced garlic
- Salt & pepper to taste

Instructions

1. Thoroughly combine the ground turkey, egg, minced garlic, salt, and pepper in a bowl. Stir in mashed avocado.
2. Make two patties out of the turkey mixture; cook for 3 mins on each side. While waiting, combine diced avocado and corn in a bowl with lemon juice, salt, and pepper. Enjoy serving with patties.

Preparing time 5 minutes, Total time 15 minutes, Servings: 1

Diabetes Cookbook

BROWN RICE WITH CHICKEN

Nutritional Info: Calories: 543cal, Total fat: 27g, Saturated fat: 5g
Protein: 32g, Carbs: 43g, Sodium: 436mg, Fiber: 6g, Sugar: 0g

Ingredients

- 1 tbsp. olive oil
- ½ of a chicken breast fillets, without bone and skin
- ½ medium onion, cut into 4 wedges
- 1 orange bell pepper, seedless and sliced thickly
- ¼ tsp. crushed garlic
- 50g brown rice
- 200g canned chopped tomatoes
- 150ml low-sodium chicken stock
- 2 tbsp. ready-made pesto

Instructions

1. Set the oven's temperature to 390F. In the deep pan, heat oil; add chicken, cook for 3–4 minutes, flip, and cook until golden. Remove meat and place aside. Cook onion, peppers, and garlic for 3–4 minutes.
2. Add the rice, tomatoes, chicken stock, and rice. Increase the stove heat and take a boil. Remove from the pan and bake for 20 minutes in the oven. Before serving, season to taste and drizzle the pesto on top.

Preparing time 10 minutes, Total time 30 minutes, Servings: 1

CHICKEN BREAST WITH APPLE SAUCE

Nutritional Info: Calories: 309cal, Total fat: 13g, Saturated fat: 3g
Protein: 25g, Carbs: 23g, Sodium: 458mg, Fiber: 3g, Sugar: 7g

Ingredients

- 1 chicken breast, skin removed
- Salt and black pepper
- ¾ tsp. canola oil
- 2 tbsp. apple juice
- 2 tbsp. chopped onion
- 2 tbsp. barbecue sauce
- ¼ tsp. minced garlic
- ½ of a small apple, sliced

Instructions

1. Rub chicken with salt and pepper. Cook the chicken in oil until brown. Stir juice, onion, chicken, barbecue sauce, and garlic into the cooker. Close the pressure-release valve and cover. Cook for 10 minutes in a high-pressure setting. After cooking, release pressure. Keep chicken warm after removal.
2. Choose the sauté option, then lower the heat. Add the apple slices and simmer for 10 minutes while stirring continuously. Serve alongside chicken.

Preparing time 25 minutes, Total time 45 minutes, Servings: 1

Diabetes Cookbook

CHICKEN BREAST AND BROCCOLI WITH DILL SAUCE

Nutritional Info: Calories: 289cal, Total fat: 9g, Saturated fat: 2g Protein: 39g, Carbs: 13g, Sodium: 620mg, Fiber: 2g, Sugar: 4g

Ingredients

- 1 chicken breast, without bone and skin
- Salt and pepper to taste
- ¾ tsp. olive oil
- 1 cup fresh broccoli florets
- ¼ cup chicken broth
- 1 tsp. all-purpose flour
- ¾ tsp. snipped fresh dill
- ¼ cup low-fat milk

Instructions

1. Rub chicken with salt and pepper. Brown chicken in oil over medium heat. Remove from pan. Add broccoli with broth; take a boil. Reduce the stove heat; cover and simmer for 3-5 minutes. Remove broccoli from pan, reserving broth.
2. Keep broccoli warm. In a deep pan, add flour, dill, milk, and broth, mix until smooth; take a boil, then simmer for 1-2 minutes. Add chicken; cook for 10-12 minutes. Serve with broccoli.

Preparing time 10 minutes, Total time 30 minutes, Servings: 1

CHICKEN BREAST WITH SPANISH AND CAULIFLOWER

Nutritional Info: Calories: 231cal, Total fat: 7g, Saturated fat: 1g Protein: 28g, Carbs: 14g, Sodium: 492mg, Fiber: 5g, Sugar: 6g

Ingredients

- ½ small head cauliflower, cut into bite-size pieces
- ¼ lb. chicken breasts, without bone and skin, cubed
- Salt and black pepper
- ¼ tbsp. canola oil
- ½ small green pepper, chopped
- 2 tbsp. chopped onion
- ½ tsp. minced garlic
- 2 tbsp. tomato juice
- 1 tbsp. chopped fresh cilantro
- ¾ tsp. lime juice

Instructions

1. Pulse cauliflower in a food processor for rice (do not overprocess). Rub chicken with salt and pepper. Cook chicken breast in oil over medium-high heat for 5 minutes. Add green pepper, onion, and garlic; cook and stir for 3 minutes.
2. Stir in tomato juice and take a boil. Add rice; cover and cook over medium heat for 7-10 minutes. Stir in cilantro and lime juice.

Preparing time 10 minutes, Total time 30 minutes, Servings: 1

Diabetes Cookbook

BAKED CHICKEN WITH TOMATO SAUCE

Nutritional Info: Calories: 293cal, Total fat: 13g, Saturated fat: 4g
Protein: 34g, Carbs: 10g, Sodium: 602mg, Fiber: 2g, Sugar: 6g

Ingredients

- ½ tbsp. minced fresh thyme
- Salt and black pepper to taste
- ¼ lb. chicken breast
- ½ cup tomato sauce
- 1 tbsp. lemon juice

Instructions

1. Preheat the oven to 425°F. Mix thyme, salt, pepper, and half of the tomato sauce in a deep bowl and rub the tomato mixture over the chicken. Place on the greased rack baking pan.
2. Bake for about 15 minutes. Add the leftover tomato sauce with lemon juice and pour over the chicken; bake for 2-3 minutes. Serve with rice or bread.

Preparing time 10 minutes, Total time 30 minutes, Servings 1

DIJON BAKED CHICKEN

Nutritional Info: Calories: 162cal, Total fat: 6g, Saturated fat: 4g
Protein: 23g, Carbs: 4g, Sodium: 684mg, Fiber: 1g, Sugar: 2g

Ingredients

- ¼ lb. chicken breasts, without skin and bone, striped
- 1/8 tsp. crushed dried rosemary
- 1/8 tsp. dried thyme
- Salt and black pepper to taste
- ¼ tbsp. coconut oil
- 2 tbsp. chopped onion
- ¼ tsp. minced garlic
- 2 tbsp. Dijon mustard

Instructions

1. Rub seasoning over chicken. Cook the chicken for 10 mins in a skillet with oil that has been heated to medium heat. Add onion, garlic, cook; stir for 5 minutes.
2. After 5 minutes of stirring in the mustard and syrup, the chicken should no longer be pink.

Preparing time 10 minutes, Total time 30 minutes, Servings 1

Diabetes Cookbook

CHICKEN WITH MUSHROOM

**Nutritional Info: Calories: 227cal, Total fat: 7g, Saturated fat: 2g
Protein: 36g, Carbs: 5g, Sodium: 381mg, Fiber: 1g, Sugar: 2g**

Ingredients

- 1 chicken breast, without skin and bone, halved
- Salt and black pepper
- ¼ tbsp. olive oil
- ½ cup sliced baby portobello mushrooms
- 2 tbsp. chopped onion
- ½ tbsp. minced garlic
- 2 tbsp. dry white wine

Instructions

1. Pound chicken breasts with a meat mallet; sprinkle with salt and pepper. Heat in a skillet over medium heat. Cook chicken for 12 minutes, and flip after halftime.
2. Take out of the pan and keep warm. Add the onion with mushrooms to the pan and stir-fry for two to three minutes. Add the garlic and stir the mixture for 30 seconds.
3. Wine is added; bring to a boil. Cook until the liquid has slightly reduced; spoon over chicken.

Preparing time 10 minutes, Total time 25 minutes, Servings 1

CHICKEN THIGHS WITH SPINACH

**Nutritional Info: Calories: 210cal, Total fat: 10g, Saturated fat: 3g
Protein: 23g, Carbs: 7g, Sodium: 360mg, Fiber: 1g, Sugar: 2g**

Ingredients

- 1 chicken thighs, without bone and skin
- Salt and black pepper to taste
- ¼ tsp. olive oil
- 1 tbsp. reduced-sodium chicken broth
- 1¾ oz. fresh spinach, trimmed
- ¾ tbsp. low-fat sour cream

Instructions

1. Rub chicken with salt and pepper. In a skillet, add oil, and put it over medium heat. Add chicken; cook for 6 mins on each side. Remove from pan; keep warm. In the same pan, add wine; take a boil.
2. Cook until wine is reduced by half. Add spinach with salt, cook; stir just until spinach is wilted. Stir in sour cream; serve the chicken with brown rice or pasta.

Preparing time 10 minutes, Total time 25 minutes, Servings: 1

CHICKEN NUGGETS

**Nutritional Info: Calories: 227cal, Total fat: 10g, Saturated fat: 3g
Protein: 23g, Carbs: 3g, Sodium: 360mg, Fiber: 1g, Sugar: 2g**

Ingredients

- ½ tbsp. all-purpose flour
- Salt and pepper
- 1/8 tsp. poultry seasoning
- 1/8 tsp. ground mustard
- 1/8 tsp. paprika
- ¼ lb. chicken breasts, without skin and bone
- ½ tbsp. canola oil

Instructions

1. Mix the first 6 ingredients in a deep dish. Flatten the chicken to the thickness of 1/2 inch.
2. Add chicken pieces to the dish and turn to coat. Cook the chicken in oil for 8 minutes until the meat is no longer pink.

Preparing time 10 minutes, Total time 25 minutes, Servings 1

SAUCY MEDITERRANEAN CHICKEN

Nutritional Info: Calories: 228cal, Total fat: 13g, Saturated fat: 2g

Ingredients

- 3 tbsp. water
- ¾ tbsp. tomato paste
- ½ tbsp. lemon juice
- Salt and pepper to taste
- A big pinch of ginger garlic powder
- Pinch of ground turmeric
- ¾ tbsp. olive oil
- 2 tbsp. chopped onion
- ¼ lb. chicken breasts, without skin and bone, cubed

Instructions

1. In a bowl, add water, tomato paste, lemon juice, salt, ginger garlic powder, and turmeric and mix until smooth. Add oil to a skillet and put it over a medium-high flame.
2. Add onions and fry until they are soft. Add chicken and stir; cook for 3–4 minutes. Add water mixture up to a boil. Simmer for 8–10 minutes on low heat. Serve with rice.

Preparing time 10 minutes, Total time 25 minutes, Servings 1

Diabetes Cookbook

SPINACH AND COTTAGE STUFFED CHICKEN

Nutritional Info: Calories: 240cal, Total fat: 14g, Saturated fat: 5g
Protein: 26g, Carbs: 2.5g, Sodium: 601mg, Fiber: 2g, Sugar: 2g

Ingredients

- 4 oz. fresh spinach
- ¾ tsp. cider vinegar
- Salt and pepper
- 1 chicken thigh, without skin and bone
- ¼ tsp. chicken seasoning
- ¾ tbsp. low-fat crumbled cottage cheese
- 1 tsp. olive oil

Instructions

1. Set the oven's temperature to 375 degrees F. Cook spinach in a skillet at medium-high heat until wilted. Add vinegar, salt, and pepper; stir; allow to cool slightly. Pound the chicken thighs with a mallet before seasoning them.
2. Add cheese and the spinach mixture to the chicken. From the long side, roll up the chicken. Cook chicken until brown thoroughly. Now bake for 15 mins. Enjoy with spinach on the side.

Preparing time 10 minutes, Total time 30 minutes, Servings: 1

CREAMY CHICKEN WITH WHITE SAUCE

Nutritional Info: Calories: 253cal, Total fat: 5g, Saturated fat: 2g
Protein: 27g, Carbs: 4.5g, Sodium: 575mg, Fiber: 0g, Sugar: 3g

Ingredients

- 1 chicken breast halves, without skin and bone
- 3½ oz. reduced-sodium chicken broth
- ¼ tbsp. all-purpose flour
- 2 tbsp. reduced-fat sour cream
- 1/8 tsp. dried parsley flakes
- Salt and black pepper
- Pinch of dill weed
- Pinch of dried thyme

Instructions

1. Place chicken breasts in a skillet with half of the broth. Cover and simmer for 10-12 minutes, turning once. Keep warm after removing the chicken from the pan. Stir the leftover broth into the pan, bring it to a boil, and then turn down the heat.
2. Combine the flour and sour cream in a small bowl. Stir into the pan. Add the onion, salt, pepper, dill weed, parsley, and salt and pepper to taste. For about 5 minutes, simmer, uncovered, until just slightly thickened.

Preparing time 10 minutes, Total time 30 minutes, Servings: 1

Diabetes Cookbook

CHICKEN BROCCOLI STIR-FRY

Nutritional Info: Calories: 190cal, **Total fat:** 6g, **Saturated fat:** 1g
Protein: 25g, **Carbs:** 9g, **Sodium:** 455mg, **Fiber:** 3g, **Sugar:** 2g

Ingredients

- ¼ tsp. cornstarch
- ¼ tbsp. cold water
- ¾ tsp. olive oil, divided
- ¼ lb. chicken breasts, without skin and bone, cubed
- ½ tsp. minced garlic
- ½ tbsp. low-sodium soy sauce
- Salt and pepper
- 4 oz. frozen broccoli

Instructions

1. Mix cornstarch and water in a bowl. Stir-fry the chicken and garlic for one minute in a skillet with half of the oil over medium-high heat. Stir in salt, pepper, and soy sauce; cook for 2–3 minutes. Remove from the pan.
2. Stir-fry vegetables for 4-5 minutes in the same pan with the leftover oil. Chicken back into the pan. Add cornstarch mixture; heat to a boil after stirring. For about a minute, cook and stir until thickened. Enjoy after serving.

Preparing time 10 minutes, Total time 30 minutes, Servings 1

POACHED CHICKEN BREAST

Nutritional Info: Calories: 200cal, **Total fat:** 4g, **Saturated fat:** 1g
Protein: 34g, **Carbs:** 2g, **Sodium:** 141mg, **Fiber:** 0g, **Sugar:** 0g

Ingredients

- 1 chicken breast half, without skin and bone
- 2 tbsp. low-sodium chicken broth
- Salt and pepper
- 1 thyme sprigs
- ½ tsp. smashed garlic
- 1 bay leaf
- water

Instructions

1. In a skillet, add chicken with wine, salt, and leftover ingredients; add cold water to cover by 1 in. Take a boil.
2. Reduce the stove heat to low, cover; simmer for 15-20 minutes. Serve with salad or rice.

Preparing time 5 minutes, Total time 25 minutes, Servings 1

Diabetes Cookbook

PROSCIUTTO WRAPPED CREAM CHEESE CHICKEN BREAST

Nutritional Info: Calories: 270cal, Total fat: 11.5g, Saturated fat: 8g
Protein: 39g, Carbs: 2.5g, Sodium: 934mg, Fiber: 0g, Sugar: 2g

Ingredients

- 1 chicken breast
- 1½ oz. finely sliced prosciutto
- 1¼ oz. low-fat cream cheese
- 4 fresh basil leaves
- Black pepper

Instructions

1. Spread cream evenly onto the prosciutto. Spread cream cheese, then place the fresh basil leaves on top to cover the cream cheese.
2. Gently wrap the prosciutto around the chicken breast and grind a little pepper on top. Bake in the oven for 25-30 minutes at 375F. Cool before serving.

Preparing time 5 minutes, Total time 30 minutes, Servings: 1

SHREDDED CHICKEN CHILI

Nutritional Info: Calories: 252cal, Total fat: 12g, Saturated fat: 2g
Protein: 30g, Carbs: 6g, Sodium: 540mg, Fiber: 4g, Sugar: 3g

Ingredients

- ½ tsp. vegetable oil
- 2 tbsp. chopped onion
- ¼ tbsp. minced garlic
- 1/8 tsp. ground cumin
- 1/8 tsp. oregano
- ¼ lb. chicken breasts, without bone & skin
- 2 oz. salsa Verde
- ½ tbsp. chopped spring onion

Instructions

1. In the instant pot, add vegetable oil and cook the onion for three minutes. Oregano, cumin, and garlic are added; stir for two minutes. Add half the salsa Verde to the pot. Add chicken breasts on top, then cover with the leftover salsa Verde.
2. Put the pot away. For ten minutes, set the timer. Then, let the pressure go naturally. Shred the chicken with a fork. Add spring onions, and then serve.

Preparing time 10 minutes, Total time 30 minutes, Servings: 1

Diabetes Cookbook

OVEN-BAKED CHICKEN MEATBALLS

Nutritional Info: Calories: 253cal, Total fat: 23g, Saturated fat: 6g Protein: 34g, Carbs: 1g, Sodium: 445mg, Fiber: 0g, Sugar: 0g

Ingredients

- 170g ground chicken breast
- 1/8 tsp. garlic powder
- Salt and pepper to taste
- 1/8 tsp. onion powder
- ¼ tbsp. olive oil
- ¼ tsp. Italian season
- 1 tbsp. grated Parmesan
- 1 small egg white

Instructions

1. Set the oven's temperature to 400 °F. Use the silicone baking sheet to arrange the baking pan. Grease, then place aside. To the bowl, add all the ingredients.
2. After thoroughly combining everything, give the mixture a few minutes to rest. Then divide into three meatballs and place on a baking sheet. Bake for 30 minutes.

Preparing time 5 minutes, Total time 35 minutes, Servings 1

GRILLED CHICKEN BREAST

Nutritional Info: Calories: 253cal, Total fat: 23g, Saturated fat: 6g Protein: 34g, Carbs: 6g, Sodium: 445mg, Fiber: 0g, Sugar: 0g

Ingredients

- 4 oz. chicken breast, without skin and bone
- 1 tbsp. olive oil
- 2 tbsp. balsamic vinegar
- ¼ tbsp. minced garlic
- 1/8 tsp. dry parsley
- ¼ tsp. dry rosemary
- Pinch of dry sage
- ¼ tsp. dry thyme
- Salt and ground pepper

Instructions

1. Put the chicken in a bag with a zip top. Combine the remaining ingredients in a bowl, then pour over the chicken. Marinade for at least two hours with a tightly sealed bag.
2. Throw away any leftover marinade. Warm the grill to medium heat. Grill for 10 minutes on each side. Slice, serve, and take pleasure.

Preparing time 5 minutes, Total time 35 minutes, Servings 1

Diabetes Cookbook

AIR FRIED CHICKEN THIGH

Nutritional Info: Calories: 284cal, Total fat: 18g, Saturated fat: 5g
Protein: 31g, Carbs: 1.5g, Sodium: 166mg, Fiber: 0g, Sugar: 0g

Ingredients

- 1 chicken thigh, bone-in, skin-off
- Salt and ground black pepper to taste
- ¼ tsp. garlic powder
- Big pinch of onion powder
- Big pinch of dried Italian seasoning
- ¼ tsp. smoked paprika powder

Instructions

1. Set the oven's to 380°F. Add chicken thighs in a sealable bag and leave aside. Combine salt, pepper, Italian seasoning, garlic, onion, and smoked paprika in a bowl. Shake the chicken thigh bag with the seasoning mixture to coat.
2. Spray some olive oil on the basket. The thigh should be placed in the basket and cooked for 12 minutes. For 10 minutes, flip and cook. Before serving, take the chicken out of the air fryer and let it rest for a while.

Preparing time 5 minutes, Total time 27 minutes, Servings: 1

CHICKEN & CHICKPEA STEW

Nutritional Info: Calories: 312cal, Total fat: 8g, Saturated fat: 1.5g
Protein: 27g, Carbs: 33g, Sodium: 613mg, Fiber: 6g, Sugar: 4g

Ingredients

- ½ tbsp. minced garlic
- Salt and ground pepper to taste
- 1 tbsp. lemon juice
- ¼ tsp. ground cumin
- ¼ tsp. paprika powder
- ¼ lb. chicken breasts, without skin and bone, cubed
- ¼ tbsp. extra-virgin olive oil
- 2 tbsp. chopped onion
- 3½ oz. canned no-salt-added diced tomatoes
- 3¾ oz. chickpeas, rinsed
- 1 tbsp. chopped flat-leaf parsley

Instructions

1. Add lemon juice, garlic, cumin, paprika, and pepper to the bowl. Add chicken to coat. Add oil to the skillet and put it over medium-high. Cook onion for 2-3 minutes. Add chicken and cook for 4 minutes.
2. Add salt, chickpeas, marinade liquid, and tomatoes with liquid. Cook the chicken for 7 minutes at medium heat, occasionally stirring, until it is thoroughly cooked. Serve with parsley on top.

Preparing time 5 minutes, Total time 27 minutes, Servings: 1

Diabetes Cookbook

CHICKEN STEW WITH CARROT

Nutritional Info: Calories: 214cal, Total fat: 6g, Saturated fat: 1g
Protein: 30g, Carbs: 10g, Sodium: 337mg, Fiber: 8g, Sugar: 4g

Ingredients

- ½ tsp. olive oil
- ½ of a small onion, chopped
- ½ cup sliced carrots
- ½ cup fat-free, low-sodium chicken broth
- ½ cup cooked chicken breast cubes
- Salt and pepper

Instructions

1. Add oil to the pan and put it at medium-high temperature. Add onion and stir for about 5 minutes until it turns golden brown. Add the broth and carrots and stir until boiling. Reduce the stove heat; cover and simmer for five minutes.
2. Add salt and pepper and simmer for 5 mins until veggies are tender. Cook and stir the chicken until it is fully heated. Take pasta, rice, or bread.

Preparing time 5 minutes, Total time 20 minutes, Servings 1

CHINESE CHICKEN CURRY

Nutritional Info: Calories: 216cal, Total fat: 8g, Saturated fat: 2g
Protein: 29g, Carbs: 7g, Sodium: 337mg, Fiber: 2g, Sugar: 4g

Ingredients

- 1 chicken breast, without skin, diced
- ¼ tbsp. olive oil
- 3 tbsp. Onion sliced into wedges
- ½ tsp. minced garlic
- 1-inch fresh ginger, finely grated
- ½ tsp. curry powder
- ¼ tsp. ground turmeric
- ½ cup hot chicken stock
- ½ tsp. dark soy sauce
- ¼ tsp. corn flour, dissolved in 3 tbsp. water
- 12½g frozen peas

Instructions

1. Add oil to the pan, cook the chicken until done, and then set aside. In the same pan, add leftover oil, cook onion, garlic, ginger, curry powder, and turmeric, and cook for 3 mins. Pour in stock soy sauce and boil the heat to simmer for a few minutes. Stir in corn flour mixture. Add the cooked chicken to the curry with frozen garden peas; cook for 2-3 mins. Serve and enjoy.

Preparing time 10 minutes, Total time 20 minutes, Servings 1

Diabetes Cookbook

CHICKEN CURRY

Nutritional Info: Calories: 216cal, Total fat: 10g, Saturated fat: 3g
Protein: 28g, Carbs: 6.5g, Sodium: 493mg, Fiber: 1.5g, Sugar: 2g

Ingredients

- ¼ tbsp. peanut oil
- ¼ cup chopped red onion
- ¼ tbsp. green curry paste
- ¼ cup coconut milk
- 2 tbsp. water
- 125g chicken
- 2 kaffir leaves
- ¼ tbsp. tamari
- ¼ tbsp. chili powder
- Pinch of cinnamon
- ¼ cup chopped coriander leaves

Instructions

1. Add oil to the pan. Stir-fry the green curry paste and onion slices for one minute. Add water with coconut milk to the pan and take a boil. Cook uncovered for 15–20 minutes.
2. Combine the tamari, cinnamon, and chili powder; add to the mixture. Add chopped coriander on top. Enjoy!

Preparing time 10 minutes, Total time 30 minutes, Servings 1

FISH AND SEAFOOD

RED PEPPER & COTTAGE TILAPIA

Nutritional Info: Calories: 192cal, Total fat: 4g, Saturated fat: 2g, Protein: 35g, Carbs: 2.9g, Sodium: 191mg, Fiber: 0g, Sugar: 0g

Ingredients

- 2 tbsp. grated low fat cottage cheese
- ¼ tsp. Italian seasoning
- ¼ tsp. red pepper flakes, crushes
- 1 small egg white
- 1 (6 oz weight) tilapia fillets
- Pinch of pepper

Instructions

1. Set the oven temperature to 425F. Place the egg in a deep bowl. Stir in cheese, pepper, Italian seasoning, and pepper. Dip the fillet in the egg mixture, then the cheese mixture.
2. Put the fillets in the greased baking dish, bake for 15 minutes, or until it flakes easily with a fork.

Preparing time 5 minutes, Total time 20 minutes, Servings 1

CRUMB ROASTED RED SNAPPER

Nutritional Info: Calories: 296cal, Total fat: 10g, Saturated fat: 2g, Protein: 36g, Carbs: 12g, Sodium: 498mg, Fiber: 0g, Sugar: 0g

Ingredients

- ¼ tsp. lemon-pepper seasoning
- ½ tsp. grated parmesan cheese
- 2 tbsp. dry breadcrumbs
- 1 red snapper fillets, 6 oz weight
- Salt to taste
- ½ tbsp. olive oil

Instructions

1. Mix cheese, lemon pepper, salt, and breadcrumbs in a bowl. Add fish fillet and coat them in the mixture.
2. Cook fillet in a skillet with hot oil until it flakes easily for about 4 minutes per side.

Preparing time 15 minutes, Total time 25 minutes, Servings 1

Diabetes Cookbook

SHRIMP WITH LEMON BUTTER SAUCE

Nutritional Info: Calories: 178cal, Total fat: 7g, Saturated fat: 4g, Protein: 19g, Carbs: 2.5g, Sodium: 476mg, Fiber: 0g, Sugar: 0g

Ingredients

- ½ tbsp. butter
- 1 tsp. minced garlic
- Pinch of cayenne pepper
- Salt to taste
- ¼ lb. uncooked shrimp, peeled and deveined
- ¼ tbsp. minced fresh parsley
- 1¼ tsp. lemon juice
- ½ tbsp. white wine

Instructions

1. In a microwave-safe bowl, combine garlic, cayenne, and butter, and microwave the covered dish on high.
2. Add salt, wine, lemon juice, parsley, and now. Add the shrimp and coat well. Cover, cook shrimp on high for 2–3 minutes or until they turn pink. Stir, then plate!

Preparing time 15 minutes, Total time 25 minutes, Servings 1

PISTACHIO CRUST SALOMON

Nutritional Info: Calories: 368cal, Total fat: 25g, Saturated fat: 5g Protein: 24g, Carbs: 13g, Sodium: 219mg, Fiber: 2g, Sugar: 3g

Ingredients

- 1 tbsp. low-fat sour cream
- 1¾ tbsp. dry breadcrumbs
- 1¾ tbsp. chopped pistachios
- 1¼ tbsp. minced shallots
- 1 salmon fillet, 4 oz weight
- ¼ tsp. garlic clove
- Pinch of red pepper flakes
- Pinch of grated lemon
- ½ tsp. snipped fresh
- 1/3 tbsp. prepared horseradish
- ¼ tbsp. olive oil

Instructions

1. Set the oven to 350F. Place the skin-side-down salmon in a baking dish. Pour sour cream over the fish fillet. Mix the rest of the ingredients.
2. Pat the crumb-nut mixture on top and press down. Bake for 12-15 mins or until it flakes easily.

Preparing time 10 minutes, Total time 30 minutes, Servings 1

Diabetes Cookbook

CRAB CAKES

Nutritional Info: Calories: 280cal, Total fat: 18g, Saturated fat: 5g Protein: 24g, Carbs: 7g, Sodium: 219mg, Fiber: 2g, Sugar: 3g

Ingredients

- 1 small egg white, lightly beaten
- 1 tbsp. chopped sweet red pepper
- ½ green onions, chopped
- 2 tbsp. breadcrumbs, divided
- 1 tbsp. reduced fat mayonnaise
- ¼ tbsp. lemon juice
- Pinch of garlic powder
- Pinch of cayenne pepper
- ½ can (3 oz weight) crabmeat
- ¼ tbsp. butter

Instructions

1. Mix the crab meat, mayonnaise, green onions, red pepper, cayenne, garlic powder, and half of the breadcrumbs. Add the last batch of breadcrumbs to the bowl. Separate mixture into 2 balls.
2. Shape them into ½-inch-thick patties after lightly coating them in breadcrumbs. In a skillet, warm oil, and cook the crab cakes for 3–4 minutes on each side until golden.

Preparing time 10 minutes, Total time 30 minutes, Servings: 1

LEMONY PARSLEY BAKED COD

Nutritional Info: Calories: 154cal, Total fat: 4g, Saturated fat: 1g Protein: 27g, Carbs: 2.5g, Sodium: 95mg, Fiber: 1g, Sugar: 0g

Ingredients

- ½ garlic cloves, minced
- ¼ tbsp. olive oil
- ¼ tbsp. grated lemon zest
- ½ tbsp. lemon juice
- ¾ tbsp. fresh parsley, minced
- Salt and pepper to taste
- ½ of a green onion, chopped
- 1 cod fillet, 6 oz weight

Instructions

1. Set the oven's temperature to 400F. Add the first seven elements to the bowl and mix well.
2. Place the fillet in a baking dish with the parsley mixture. Bake for 10-15 minutes.

Preparing time 10 minutes, Total time 25 minutes, Servings: 1

Diabetes Cookbook

TUNA LETTUCE WRAPS

Nutritional Info: Calories: 285cal, Total fat: 13g, Saturated fat: 2g Protein: 22g, Carbs: 20g, Sodium: 421mg, Fiber: 7g, Sugar: 1g

Ingredients

- 2 tbsp. chopped red onion
- 3¾ oz. canned cannellini beans, rinsed and drained
- 3 oz. canned tuna in water, drained and flaked
- ½ tbsp. olive oil
- ¼ tbsp. minced fresh parsley
- ½ small ripe avocado, peeled and sliced
- 3 lettuce leaves
- Salt and pepper to taste

Instructions

1. Add onion, cannellini beans, oil, chopped parsley, salt, and pepper to the deep bowl. Toss to coat, place over lettuce leaves, top with avocado. Serve and enjoy.

Preparing time 10 minutes, Total time 15 minutes, Servings: 1

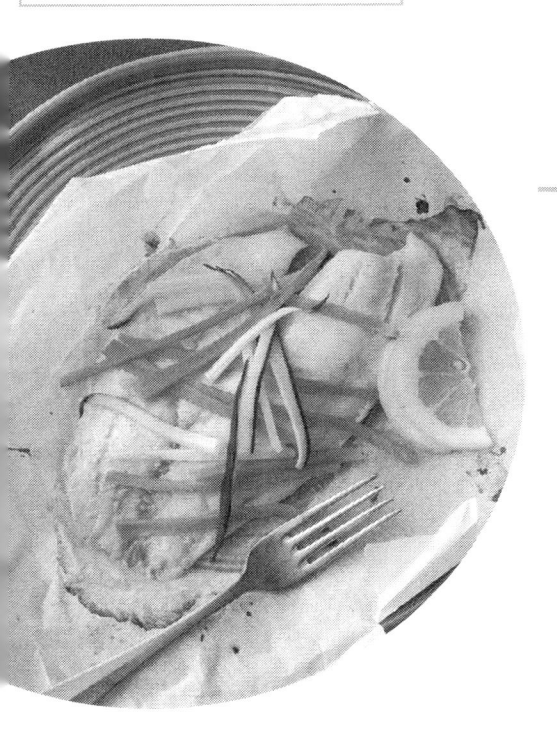

ORANGE TILAPIA IN PARCHMENT

Nutritional Info: Calories: 166cal, Total fat: 2g, Saturated fat: 1g Protein: 32g, Carbs: 6g, Sodium: 220mg, Fiber: 1g, Sugar: 2g

Ingredients

- Salt and pepper to taste
- Pinch of cayenne pepper
- 1 tbsp. orange juice
- 1 tsp. grated orange zest
- 2 tbsp. julienned zucchini
- 2 tbsp. julienned carrot
- 1 tilapia fillet, 6 oz weight

Instructions

1. Set the oven to 450F. Add orange juice, zest, salt, pepper, and cayenne pepper to the small bowl, mix well and leave aside.
2. Put a fillet on the parchment paper, then add some zucchini and carrots. Drizzle the mixture of orange juice over everything. Bake for 14-15 mins.

Preparing time 10 minutes, Total time 15 minutes, Servings: 1

Diabetes Cookbook

PARMESAN BAKED COD

Nutritional Info: Calories: 243cal, Total fat: 15g, Saturated fat: 2g Protein: 20g, Carbs: 6g, Sodium: 500mg, Fiber: 0g, Sugar: 2g

Ingredients

- 1 cod fillet
- 1 tbsp. grated low-fat parmesan cheese
- 2½ tbsp. low-fat mayonnaise
- ¼ tsp. Worcestershire Sauce
- 1 spring onions, chopped

Instructions

1. Set the oven to 400°F. Place cod in a square baking dish, greased with cooking spray.
2. Cover fillets with a mixture of the remaining ingredients. Uncover, and bake for 17-20 mins, or until fish flakes easily with a work.

Preparing time 10 minutes, Total time 30 minutes, Servings: 1

CAJUN SHRIMP

Nutritional Info: Calories: 150cal, Total fat: 5.5g, Saturated fat: 0.9g Protein: 23g, Carbs: 2g, Sodium: 786mg, Fiber: 0g, Sugar: 0g

Ingredients

- ¼ tbsp. olive oil
- ½ tsp. minced garlic
- ¼ lb. large shrimp peeled and deveined
- ¼ tbsp. Cajun seasoning

Instructions

1. Add oil to the skillet and put it over medium-high heat. Include the garlic. Add the Cajun seasoning and shrimp, and then coat everything with butter.
2. Cook the shrimp for 3-5 minutes until they are opaque and thoroughly cooked.

Preparing time 10 minutes, Total time 30 minutes, Servings: 1

Diabetes Cookbook

LEMON-PEPPER TILAPIA

Nutritional Info: Calories: 180cal, Total fat: 5g, Saturated fat: 3g Protein: 32g, Carbs: 1.5g, Sodium: 254mg, Fiber: 0g, Sugar: 0g

Ingredients

- 1 tilapia fillet, 6 oz weight
- Salt and pepper to taste
- ½ tbsp. olive
- ¼ tsp. paprika
- ½ tbsp. grated lemon zest
- ¼ tbsp. lemon juice
- 1 tbsp. minced fresh parsley

Instructions

1. Set the oven to 425F. Put tilapia in the baking pan. Melt olive oil in the microwave, then add the lemon juice and zest. Drizzle over the fish and season with salt, pepper, and paprika.
2. Uncover, bake for 12 minutes, or until fish flake easily with a fork. Add parsley as a garnish.

Preparing time 10 minutes, Total time 20 minutes, Servings 1

COD WITH STUFFED OLIVES

Nutritional Info: Calories: 171cal, Total fat: 3g, Saturated fat: 0g Protein: 27g, Carbs: 6g, Sodium: 598mg, Fiber: 0g, Sugar: 1g

Ingredients

- 1 cod fillet, 6 oz weight
- ¼ shallot, thinly sliced
- ¼ tsp. dried oregano
- 1¼ tbsp. garlic-stuffed olives, halved
- Salt and pepper to taste
- ½ tbsp. water
- ¼ medium lemon, thinly sliced
- ½ tbsp. olive juice

Instructions

1. Grease a skillet with cooking spray and add the fillet to it. Top with lemon and shallot after adding salt and oregano.
2. Spread olive around the fish, then add water and olive juice and take a boil. Decrease the stove heat, cover; cook for 8 to 10 minutes.

Preparing time 10 minutes, Total time 25 minutes, Servings 1

Diabetes Cookbook

SPINACH AND SHRIMP

Nutritional Info: Calories: 205cal, Total fat: 9g, Saturated fat: 1g Protein: 22g, Carbs: 9g, Sodium: 727mg, Fiber: 4g, Sugar: 6g

Ingredients

- ½ tbsp. olive oil
- ¾ tbsp. minced fresh basil
- ¼ of a medium onion
- ¼ tsp. dried oregano
- ½ tbsp. minced garlic
- Salt and pepper to taste
- 4 tbsp. dry white wine
- ¼ lb. uncooked shrimp
- 1 can tomato sauce
- ¾ cup finely chopped fresh spinach

Instructions

1. Add olive to the skillet. Add onion; stir-fry for 5-7 minutes, or until it is soft. Add the garlic and cook for 2 mins. Stir in the wine, take a boil, and continue cooking until the liquid is halved. Add salt, pepper, basil, and tomato sauce after stirring.
2. Cook and stir the sauce for 10 minutes or until it slightly thickens. Add the shrimp and spinach; cook and stir for 3 to 5 minutes, or until the shrimp turn pink and the spinach wilts. Cheese can be added if desired.

Preparing time 10 minutes, Total time 30 minutes, Servings 1

SPICED SALMON

Nutritional Info: Calories: 208cal, Total fat: 13g, Saturated fat: 3g Protein: 23g, Carbs: 2g, Sodium: 392mg, Fiber: 1g, Sugar: 7g

Ingredients

- Salt to taste
- 1 tsp. chili powder
- Pinch of ground cinnamon
- ½ tsp. grated lemon zest
- 1 salmon fillet, 4 oz weight
- Pinch of ground cumin

Instructions

1. Set the oven to 350F. Combine all ingredients (except salmon); rub over salmon.
2. Put the object in a baking dish with cooking spray on it. Bake for about 17-20 mins until it flakes easily.

Preparing time 10 minutes, Total time 30 minutes, Servings 1

Diabetes Cookbook

TOMATO TUNA SALAD

Nutritional Info: Calories: 248cal, **Total fat:** 16g, **Saturated fat:** 3g **Protein:** 22g, **Carbs:** 4g, **Sodium:** 656mg, **Fiber:** 2g, **Sugar:** 7g

Ingredients

- 2¾ tbsp. low-fat mayonnaise
- Black pepper to taste
- 2 tbsp. chopped sweet onion
- ¼ can white tuna in water, drained and flaked
- ¼ celery rib, chopped
- ¼ tsp. minced fresh parsley

Instructions

1. Add low-fat mayonnaise, onion, celery, minced parsley, and pepper to the bowl. Stir in tuna.
2. Serve the tuna mixture with tomato wedges.

Preparing time 5 minutes, Total time 15 minutes, Servings 1

TILAPIA FISH TACOS

Nutritional Info: Calories: 332cal, **Total fat:** 16g, **Saturated fat:** 2g **Protein:** 33g, **Carbs:** 14g, **Sodium:** 663mg, **Fiber:** 3g, **Sugar:** 1g

Ingredients

- ½ cup coleslaw mix
- ¼ tsp. ground cumin
- 2 tbsp. chopped fresh cilantro
- Salt and pepper to taste
- ½ of a green onion, sliced
- ½ tsp. chopped jalapeno pepper, seedless
- 1 tilapia fillet
- 2 tsp. canola oil
- ½ of a small ripe avocado
- 1 tsp. lime juice

Instructions

1. To the bowl, add the first four ingredients. Add half the oil, the lime juice, the cumin, and the salt and pepper to taste. Keep chilled until servings.
2. Rub the leftover salt and pepper into the fillet. Cook tilapia in the remaining oil for 3 to 4 minutes on each side, or until the fish flake easily with a fork. Add avocado and slaw on top.

Preparing time 5 minutes, Total time 15 minutes, Servings 1

Diabetes Cookbook

COD WITH BACON AND TOMATOES

Nutritional Info: Calories: 178cal, Total fat: 6g, Saturated fat: 2g Protein: 26g, Carbs: 5g, Sodium: 485mg, Fiber: 1g, Sugar: 4g

Ingredients

- 1 center-cut bacon strip, chopped
- Salt and pepper to taste
- 1 cod fillet
- ½ cup grape tomatoes, halved
- ¼ tbsp. balsamic vinegar

Instructions

1. Cook bacon until it is crispy. Drain on a paper towel. Season the fillet with salt and pepper. Add the fillets to the bacon drippings and cook for 4-6 minutes on each side over medium-high heat. Remove and keep warm.
2. Add tomatoes to the skillet; cook for 2-4 minutes. Add vinegar and turn down the heat to medium. Cook more for 1-2 mins or until the sauce thickens. Bacon and tomato mixture goes well with cod.

Preparing time 10 minutes, Total time 25 minutes, Servings: 1

CILANTRO LIME SHRIMP

Nutritional Info: Calories: 167cal, Total fat: 8g, Saturated fat: 1g Protein: 19g, Carbs: 4g, Sodium: 284mg, Fiber: 0g, Sugar: 1g

Ingredients

- 1¼ tbsp. chopped fresh cilantro
- Salt and pepper to taste
- ¼ tsp. grated lime zest
- Pinch of ground cumin
- 1¼ tbsp. lime juice
- ¼ jalapeno pepper, seedless and minced
- ¼ lb. uncooked shrimp
- ½ tbsp. olive oil
- ¼ tbsp. minced garlic
- Lime slices

Instructions

1. Add all ingredients (except shrimp) to the bowl, toss in shrimp and let stand 15mins. Thread shrimp and lime slice onto metal or soaked wooden skewers.
2. Grill shrimp over moderate heat until they turn pink, 2-4 mins per side.

Preparing time 10 minutes, Total time 30 minutes, Servings: 1

Diabetes Cookbook

PAN FRIED SHRIMP AND MUSHROOMS

Nutritional Info: Calories: 132cal, Total fat: 3g, Saturated fat: 1g Protein: 20g, Carbs: 6g, Sodium: 258mg, Fiber: 1g, Sugar: 2g

Ingredients

- 1 garlic clove, minced
- ¼ cup sliced green onions
- ½ tsp. canola oil
- 1 tbsp. chicken broth
- ¼ lb. uncooked shrimp
- ¾ cup sliced fresh mushroom

Instructions

1. Sauté garlic in oil for one minute in a pan. Stir in shrimp, mushrooms, and onions.
2. Cook for 2 more minutes, stirring occasionally, or until the shrimp turn pink. Lemon garnish served with rice.

Preparing time 10 minutes, Total time 15 minutes, Servings: 1

TEQUILA LIME SHRIMP ZOODLES

Nutritional Info: Calories: 246cal, Total fat: 14g, Saturated fat: 6g Protein: 20g, Carbs: 7g, Sodium: 258mg, Fiber: 1g, Sugar: 3g

Ingredients

- 1 tbsp. olive oil
- ¼ lb. uncooked shrimp
- ¼ shallot minced
- ½ of a medium zucchini, spiralized
- ¼ tbsp. minced garlic
- 1 tbsp. tequila
- Salt and pepper to taste
- ¼ tsp. grated lime zest
- ½ tbsp. lime juice
- 1 tbsp. minced fresh parsley

Instructions

1. In a skillet, add ¾ tbsp oil and put it over medium heat. Add garlic, shallot; cook for 1-2 minutes. Remove from heat, and add tequila, lime juice, and zest. Cook for 2-3 mins at moderate heat or until the liquid almost completely evaporates.
2. Zucchini and shrimp are stirred in with the remaining olive oil. Add salt and pepper to taste. Cook for 4-5 mins. Add more lime zest and parsley on top.

Preparing time 10 minutes, Total time 30 minutes, Servings: 1

Diabetes Cookbook

SWEET PEPPER COD

Nutritional Info: Calories: 168cal, Total fat: 1g, Saturated fat: 0g Protein: 29g, Carbs: 11g, Sodium: 398mg, Fiber: 2g, Sugar: 4g

Ingredients

- ¼ of a medium onion, halved and sliced
- ¼ cup low-sodium chicken broth
- ¼ tbsp. lemon juice
- ½ tbsp. minced garlic
- ¼ tsp. dried oregano
- ½ tsp. grated lemon zest
- ½ small lemon, halved and sliced
- Salt to taste
- ¼ cup julienned green and red pepper
- ½ tsp. cornstarch
- ¼ tbsp. cold water
- 1 cod fillet, 4 oz weight

Instructions

1. Add the first 7 ingredients to the skillet and take a boil Cover and lower the heat: simmer for 6-8 mins. Over the onion mixture, spread the fish and peppers. For 6-9 mins, cover, and simmer.
2. Keep fish and vegetables warm after removal. Mix cornstarch with water; add to skillet gradually. Take a boil; cook for 2 mins or until thickened. Serve fish and vegetables on a plate. Add lemon to the dish.

Preparing time 10 minutes, Total time 25 minutes, Servings: 1

SALMON AND VEGGIES

Nutritional Info: Calories: 383cal, Total fat: 23g, Saturated fat: 9g Protein: 31g, Carbs: 13g, Sodium: 388mg, Fiber: 2g, Sugar: 4g

Ingredients

- 375g salmon fillet
- Salt and pepper to taste
- 2 tbsp. olive oil
- ¼ lb. fresh asparagus, trimmed
- ½ tbsp. balsamic vinegar
- 1 medium sweet red pepper, cut into 1-inch pieces
- ½ tsp. minced fresh rosemary
- ¼ tsp. minced garlic

Instructions

1. Set the oven temperature to 400F. Put the salmon in the baking dish. Add salt, rosemary, garlic, vinegar, and oil to the bowl. Rub half into the oil mixture over the salmon. In a bowl, add asparagus and red pepper.
2. Drizzle with half of the oil mixture and toss to combine. Sprinkle pepper all around the salmon in the pan. Bake the fish and veggies for 15 minutes.

Preparing time 10 minutes, Total time 30 minutes, Servings: 1

Diabetes Cookbook

TUNA KABOBS

Nutritional Info: Calories: 230cal, Total fat: 2g, Saturated fat: 0g Protein: 29g, Carbs: 24g, Sodium: 50mg, Fiber: 4g, Sugar: 12g

Ingredients

- 2 tbsp. frozen corn, thawed
- 1 green onions, chopped
- ¼ tsp. coarsely ground pepper
- ¼ jalapeno pepper, seedless and chopped
- ½ sweet red peppers, sliced
- ½ tbsp. coarsely chopped fresh parsley
- ½ tbsp. lime juice
- ¼ medium mango, peeled and cubed
- ¼ lb. tuna steaks, cubed
- Black pepper

Instructions

1. To the bowl, add the first five ingredients for the salsa; set aside. Rub pepper over tuna. Thread red peppers, tuna, and mango onto a metal or soaked wooden skewer.
2. Put the skewers on the grill rack. Cover, cook over moderate heat for 10-12 mins, or until peppers are tender and tuna is slightly pink in the center.

Preparing time 10 minutes, Total time 30 minutes, Servings: 1

POACHED SALMON

Nutritional Info: Calories: 280cal, Total fat: 16g, Saturated fat: 3g Protein: 29g, Carbs: 5g, Sodium: 115mg, Fiber: 0g, Sugar: 0g

Ingredients

- ½ cup water
- ¼ tbsp. soy sauce
- ¼ of a medium onion, chopped
- 2 whole peppercorns
- 1 celery ribs, chopped
- ½ bay leaf
- 2 springs fresh parsley
- ½ salmon fillet, 6 oz weight
- ¼ cup dry white wine

Instructions

1. Add the first 8 elements to the pot. Take a boil, then turn down the heat and simmer for 30 minutes. Discard any spices and vegetables.
2. Add liquid to the slow cooker, fold salmon in foil, and place slowly.
3. Cover, and cook for 60–70 minutes on high. Take the salmon out of the cooking liquid. Serve with lemon and dill, warm or cold.

Preparing time 10 minutes, Total time 140 minutes, Servings: 1

Diabetes Cookbook

CHILI LIME WITH CRUNCHY SHRIMP

Nutritional Info: Calories: 256cal, Total fat: 13g, Saturated fat: 2g Protein: 20g, Carbs: 17g, Sodium: 315mg, Fiber: 2g, Sugar: 1g

Ingredients

- ¼ lb. uncooked shrimp
- ½ small lime
- ¼ tbsp. minced garlic
- 2 tbsp. crushed tortilla chips
- 1 tbsp. chopped fresh cilantro
- ¼ tsp. paprika powder
- ½ tbsp. olive oil
- 2 tbsp. halved cherry tomatoes
- 1 tsp. ground cumin
- ½ small ripe avocado, peeled and cubed
- Salt and pepper to taste

Instructions

1. Set the oven to 425°F. In a pan, add the first seven ingredients. Squeeze lime juice after cutting in half crosswise.
2. Toss the shrimp mixture with the zest and juice to coat. Add crushed chips, cilantro, oil, and the shrimp mixture to the bowl. Bake for 13-15 mins. Top with avocado and tomatoes.

Preparing time 10 minutes, Total time 30 minutes, Servings 1

PAN FRIED SCALLOPS

Nutritional Info: Calories: 181cal, Total fat: 9g, Saturated fat: 3g Protein: 19g, Carbs: 5g, Sodium: 524mg, Fiber: 0g, Sugar: 1g

Ingredients

- ¼ lb. sea scallops
- ¾ tbsp. orange juice
- Salt to taste
- 1 tbsp. finely chopped onion
- ¼ tsp. pepper
- ¼ tsp. dried oregano
- ¼ tbsp. olive oil
- ¼ tsp. Dijon mustard
- 2 tbsp. chicken broth
- ½ tsp. minced garlic
- ¾ tbsp. cold butter

Instructions

1. Season scallops with salt and pepper. Cook in oil until opaque and firm. Remove and keep warm. Stirring to remove browned bits from the pans, add wine to the skillet. Pour in orange juice, onion, oregano, mustard, and garlic.
2. Take a boil; cook and stir for 2–3 minutes, or until reduced by half. Remove from the heat; stir in butter and heat until butter melts.

Preparing time 10 minutes, Total time 25 minutes, Servings 1

COD WITH PEPPER AND SALSA

Nutritional Info: Calories: 178cal, **Total fat:** 7g, **Saturated fat:** 4g, **Protein:** 19g, **Carbs:** 2.5g, **Sodium:** 476mg, **Fiber:** 0g, **Sugar:** 0g

Ingredients

- 1 cod or haddock fillets
- 2 tbsp. salsa
- ½ tsp. olive oil
- ¼ cup julienned green and red pepper
- Salt to taste
- 1¼ tbsp. orange juice

Instructions

1. Set the oven range to 350F. Arrange fish in the baking dish and brush oil on both sides. Add salt and pepper to taste.
2. Top the fish with orange juice, salsa, and peppers. Cover, bake for 17–20 minutes, or until fish flakes easily with a fork.

Preparing time 10 minutes, Total time 25 minutes, Servings: 1

SEASONED TILAPIA FILLETS

Nutritional Info: Calories: 193cal, **Total fat:** 7g, **Saturated fat:** 4g **Protein:** 32g, **Carbs:** 1g, **Sodium:** 589mg, **Fiber:** 0g, **Sugar:** 0g

Ingredients

- 1 tilapia fillet
- Pinch of dried thyme
- ½ tbsp. olive oil
- Pinch of onion powder
- 1 tsp. fish seasoning
- Salt and pepper to taste
- Big pinch of dried parsley flakes
- Pinch of garlic powder

Instructions

1. Set the oven range to 425F. Arrange tilapia in the baking dish, and drizzle butter. Mix the leftover ingredients in a small bowl, then sprinkle over the fillets.
2. Bake for 10 mins. Remove the cover; continue baking for 5-8 minutes, or until the fish starts to flake easily.

Preparing time 10 minutes, Total time 25 minutes, Servings: 1

Diabetes Cookbook

SALMON STUFFED AVOCADOS

**Nutritional Info: Calories: 304cal, Total fat: 20g, Saturated fat: 3g
Protein: 23g, Carbs: 8g, Sodium: 399mg, Fiber: 7g, Sugar: 1.8g**

Ingredients

- 1/8 cup diced celery
- ½ tbsp. chopped fresh parsley
- ¼ tbsp. lime juice
- ½ tsp. low-fat mayonnaise
- ¼ tsp Dijon mustard
- Pinch of salt
- 1 tbsp. nonfat plain yogurt
- ½ of a small avocado
- 3 oz. canned salmon, drained, flaked

Instructions

1. Add celery, chopped parsley, lime juice, plain yogurt, low-fat mayonnaise, pepper, and salt to the bowl, and mix. Add salmon and mix well. Scoop 1 tbsp flesh of the avocado into a bowl.
2. Mix the avocado flesh well and stir in the salmon mixture. Fill half with the salmon mixture. Garnish with chives and serve.

Preparing time 15 minutes, Total time 20 minutes, Servings 1

CLASSIC GRILL SALMON

**Nutritional Info: Calories: 113cal, Total fat: 9g, Saturated fat: 1g
Protein: 6g, Carbs: 2g, Sodium: 15mg, Fiber: 1g, Sugar: 1g**

Ingredients

- 2 oz. salmon fillets
- Few basil leaves, chopped
- 1 tbsp. lemon juice
- ½ tbsp. olive oil
- ½ garlic clove, chopped
- ½ tsp. lemon pepper
- Cooking spray

Instructions

1. Add oil to the pan, put it over moderate heat and cook garlic for 2 minutes, or until fragrant. Add basil and sauté for 15 seconds; add the lemon juice and turn off the heat. Stir, then put aside.
2. Preheat the pan and grease with cooking spray. Season the fillets with lemon and pepper after brushing them with the garlic-lemon mixture. Grill for 10 mins; serve with your preferred vegetables.

Preparing time 5 minutes, Total time 20 minutes, Servings 1

Diabetes Cookbook

DESSERTS

CHEESECAKE BARS

**Nutritional Info: Calories: 225cal, Total fat: 9.3g, Saturated fat: 5g
Protein: 12g, Carbs: 24g, Sodium: 150mg, Fiber: 1g, Sugar: 2g**

Ingredients

- 1 tsp. grapeseed oil
- 10g monk fruit sweetener, divided
- ¾ tbsp. lemon juice, divided
- 3 tbsp. all-purpose flour
- Pinch of salt
- 2 tbsp. low-fat cream cheese
- 1 large egg white
- Pinch of grated lemon zest
- 2 fresh raspberries, halved

Instructions

1. Beat grapeseed and half of the sweetener together until smooth. Add flour and salt, then add ½ lemon juice. Into the prepared pan, press. Bake for 10 minutes, or until golden brown, at 350 degrees.
2. In the meantime, blend the cream cheeses and extra sweetener in a small bowl. Include the egg, lemon juice, and lemon zest. Pour over the crust.
3. Bake for a further 10 minutes or until the filling is set. One hour of cooling. Cut in squares, then triangles. Serve with a garnish.

Preparing time 10 minutes, Total time 30 minutes, Servings 1

BROWNIES

**Nutritional Info: Calories: 166cal, Total fat: 10.7g, Saturated fat: 1.8g
Protein: 5.4g, Carbs: 12g, Sodium: 138mg, Fiber: 2.2g, Sugar: 0.8g**

Ingredients

- 15g mashed potatoes
- 1 tbsp. monk fruit sweetener
- ½ tbsp. canola oil
- 1 small egg, lightly beaten
- 2-3 drops of vanilla extract
- 1 tbsp. all-purpose flour
- ¾ tbsp. cocoa powder
- 1/8 tsp. baking powder
- 1/8 tsp. salt

Instructions

1. Mix mashed potatoes, sweetener, oil, eggs, and vanilla in a large bowl. Combine the flour, cocoa, baking powder, and salt; gradually add to the potato mixture. Fold in pecans if desired. Transfer to a greased 9-in. square baking pan.
2. Bake at 350° until a tester inserted in the center comes out clean, 23-27 minutes. Cool on a wire rack. Dust with confectioners' sugar. Cut into bars.

Preparing time 10 minutes, Total time 35 minutes, Servings: 1

Diabetes Cookbook

GRILL PINEAPPLE

**Nutritional Info: Calories: 143cal, Total fat: 1.8g, Saturated fat: 0.2g
Protein: 1.3g, Carbs: 30.5g, Sodium: 2.4mg, Fiber: 3.3g, Sugar: 22.4g**

Ingredients

- ¼ fresh small pineapple, peeled and sliced into 2 parts
- 1 tsp. monk fruit sweetener
- 1 tsp. lime juice
- ½ tsp. olive oil
- 1/8 tsp. chili powder
- Dash of salt

Instructions

1. Peel pineapple. Cut lengthwise into 2-3 wedges; remove the core. In a small bowl, mix the remaining ingredients until blended. Brush pineapple with half of the glaze; reserve the remaining mixture for basting.
2. Grill pineapple over medium heat for 2-4 minutes on each side or until lightly browned, occasionally basting with reserved glaze.

Preparing time 5 minutes, Total time 15 minutes, Servings 1

CHOCOLATE AND AVOCADO MOUSSE

**Nutritional Info: Calories: 443cal, Total fat: 35g, Saturated fat: 12g
Protein: 7.4g, Carbs: 25g, Sodium: 28mg, Fiber: 15.6g, Sugar: 2.8g**

Ingredients

- 1 oz. chopped unsweetened chocolate chips; microwave melted
- 1 small ripe avocado, peeled, stoned, and sliced
- ¾ tbsp. unsweetened cocoa powder
- 1 tbsp. unsweetened almond milk
- ¼ tsp. pure vanilla extract
- Pinch of salt

Instructions

1. Add chocolate, cocoa powder, almond milk, vanilla extract, and salt to a high-powered food blender. Blend until very smooth and creamy.
2. Spoon into glasses. Enjoy immediately as a pudding or chilled for 2 hours. Top with fresh raspberries, serve and enjoy.

Preparing time 5 minutes, Total time 10 minutes, Servings 1

Diabetes Cookbook

VANILLA CUSTARD BERRIES

Nutritional Info: Calories: 254cal, Total fat: 16g, Saturated fat: 9g Protein: 4.6g, Carbs: 23g, Sodium: 32mg, Fiber: 0g, Sugar: 1.5g

Ingredients

- ¼ cup low-fat milk cream
- 1 small egg yolk
- 1 tsp. monk fruit sweetener
- ½ tsp. vanilla extract
- ½ cup fresh berries

Instructions

1. Add cream, egg yolks, and sweetener to a heavy saucepan, put it over low heat, cook until the mixture is thick, and easily coat the back of a metal spoon. Don't boil the water.
2. Transfer to a mixing bowl and mix in the vanilla extract. Refrigerate until chilled. Serve with fresh berries on the side.

Preparing time 10 minutes, Total time 20 minutes, Servings 1

BANANA SUNDAE

Nutritional Info: Calories: 174cal, Total fat: 6.8g, Saturated fat: 1.9g Protein: 3.6g, Carbs: 24.5g, Sodium: 34mg, Fiber: 2g, Sugar: 17g

Ingredients

- 1 frozen ripe banana, sliced
- ½ tbsp. peanut butter
- ¼ tbsp. thawed frozen light, low-fat whipped topping
- ¼ tsp. sugar-free chocolate-flavor syrup
- 1 tsp. chopped peanuts
- 1 maraschino cherry

Instructions

1. In the high-power food blender, add bananas with peanut butter. Cover and blend until almost smooth. Scoop the mixture into sundae dishes.
2. Top with whipped, sugar-free chocolate flavor syrup, peanuts, and a maraschino cherry. Serve right away.

Preparing time 10 minutes, Total time 25 minutes, Servings 1

Diabetes Cookbook

CHOCOLATE-DIPPED BANANA BITES

Nutritional Info: Calories: 527cal, Total fat: 35.4g, Saturated fat: 16g
Protein: 11g, Carbs: 42g, Sodium: 4mg, Fiber: 9g, Sugar: 16g

Ingredients

- 1 medium banana, peel, slice, and freeze for 2 hours
- 1 tbsp. peanut butter
- 3 tbsp. unsweetened chocolate chips, melted

Instructions

1. Spread peanut butter in each slice (like a sandwich), then dip the frozen banana bite in the chocolate.
2. Let stand until the chocolate is set. If not serving immediately, return to the freezer.

Preparing time 10 minutes, Total time 10 minutes, Servings: 1

WATERMELON PIZZA

Nutritional Info: Calories: 168cal, Total fat: 1.3g, Saturated fat: 0.3g
Protein: 4g, Carbs: 35g, Sodium: 24mg, Fiber: 7g, Sugar: 20g

Ingredients

- 2 tbsp. low-fat plain yogurt
- 3-4 drops of vanilla extract
- 1 small watermelon round (about 1-inch thick), center-cut
- ½ cup mixed berries
- 2 tbsp. torn fresh mint leaves

Instructions

1. Combine yogurt and vanilla drops in a small bowl. Spread 1/4 cup yogurt mixture over each slice of watermelon.
2. Cut each slice into 4 wedges. Top with strawberries, blackberries, and mint.

Preparing time 10 minutes, Total time 10 minutes, Servings: 1

Diabetes Cookbook

STRAWBERRY, CHOCOLATE, AND YOGURT BARK

**Nutritional Info: Calories: 116cal, Total fat: 5g, Saturated fat: 3.1g
Protein: 3.3g, Carbs: 14.5g, Sodium: 5mg, Fiber: 0.3g, Sugar: 13g**

Ingredients

- 4 tbsp. low-fat plain yogurt
- 3-4 drops of vanilla extract
- 2 tbsp. sliced strawberries
- ¾ tbsp. mini chocolate chips

Instructions

1. Place a parchment paper to line the baking sheet. In a bowl, combine the yogurt and vanilla extract. Spread on the rectangle baking sheet.
2. Sprinkle the chocolate chips on top and scatter the strawberries on top. Freeze for at least 3 hours, or until very firm. Cut into pieces and serve when ready to eat.

Preparing time 10 minutes, Total time 10 minutes, Servings: 1

PEANUT BUTTER BALLS

**Nutritional Info: Calories: 120cal, Total fat: 4g, Saturated fat: 0.6g
Protein: 3.3g, Carbs: 18.6g, Sodium: 43mg, Fiber: 0g, Sugar: 11.2g**

Ingredients

- 2 tbsp. natural peanut butter
- 2 tbsp. crispy rice cereal
- 2 tbsp. dark chocolate chips, melted

Instructions

1. Using parchment or wax paper, line a baking sheet. In a medium mixing bowl, combine peanut butter and cereal. Using about 2 tsp batter per ball, roll the mixture into 3-4 balls.
2. Place on the baking sheet. Freeze the balls for about 15 minutes or until they are firm. Dip the balls in chocolate. Return to the freezer for another 15 minutes to allow the chocolate to set.

Preparing time 10 minutes, Total time 10 minutes, Servings: 1

Diabetes Cookbook

PINEAPPLE SORBET

Nutritional Info: Calories: 60cal, **Total fat:** 0.2g, **Saturated fat:** 0g
Protein: 0.6g, **Carbs:** 14g, **Sodium:** 2mg, **Fiber:** 1.4g, **Sugar:** 12g

Ingredients

- 2¾ oz. frozen pineapple chunks
- 25g frozen mango chunks, peeled and chopped
- ½ tsp. lemon juice

Instructions

1. Blend pineapple, mango, and lemon juice in a food blender until smooth and creamy.
2. For the best texture, serve immediately.

Preparing time 10 minutes, Total time 10 minutes, Servings: 1

STRAWBERRY SORBET

Nutritional Info: Calories: 145cal, **Total fat:** 0.6g, **Saturated fat:** 0.1g
Protein: 2g, **Carbs:** 33g, **Sodium:** 2.3mg, **Fiber:** 5g, **Sugar:** 17.7g

Ingredients

- ¼ lb. frozen strawberries
- 1 small frozen banana
- 1 tablespoon fresh lemon juice
- ¼ cup chilled water, as needed

Instructions

1. In a food blender, all ingredients to it, and blend until smooth, about 2 minutes.
2. If necessary, add ¼ cup of cold water to achieve the desired consistency, scraping down the sides of the bowl as needed.
3. Serve right away or store in the freezer for up to 30 minutes.

Preparing time 10 minutes, Total time 10 minutes, Servings: 1

Diabetes Cookbook

CHOCOLATE CHIP COOKIES

Nutritional Info: Calories: 232cal, **Total fat:** 16g, **Saturated fat:** 3.1g
Protein: 9.8g, **Carbs:** 12.3g, **Sodium:** 57mg, **Fiber:** 2g, **Sugar:** 1.6g

Ingredients

- 1 small egg
- Salt to taste
- 1 tbsp. natural peanut butter
- 1 tsp. monk fruit sweetener
- 1 tbsp. sugar-free chocolate chips

Instructions

1. Preheat the oven to 375. Arrange two baking sheets with parchment paper. Beat egg, salt, peanut butter, sweetener, and chocolate chips in a bowl.
2. Place a tablespoon of dough on each prepared baking sheet, about 2 inches apart. Like a cookie, press and shape the dough. Bake for 8 to 10 minutes. Allow cooling for 20 minutes before serving.

Preparing time 10 minutes, Total time 40 minutes, Servings: 1

VEGAN OATMEAL COOKIES

Nutritional Info: Calories: 331cal, **Total fat:** 17.5g, **Saturated fat:** 1.3g
Protein: 8g, **Carbs:** 35.5g, **Sodium:** 11mg, **Fiber:** 5.7g, **Sugar:** 19.6g

Ingredients

- 13½g quick-cooking oats
- 12g almond flour
- Pinch of ground cinnamon
- Pinch of salt
- ½ ripe small banana, mashed
- 1¼ tbsp. almond butter
- 3-4 drops of vanilla extract
- 20g raisins

Instructions

1. Preheat the oven to 350. Arrange the baking sheet with parchment paper. Mix dry elements in a bowl. Mash banana with wet elements in the other bowl until creamy and well combined.
2. Combine dry and wet elements and raisins. Scoop a tbsp of dough into balls and press to shape like a cookie. Bake until firm and light brown on the bottom, about 15 minutes.

Preparing time 15 minutes, Total time 30 minutes, Servings: 1

WATERMELON SHERBET

**Nutritional Info: Calories: 166cal, Total fat: 10g, Saturated fat: 0g
Protein: 5.9g, Carbs: 13g, Sodium: 76mg, Fiber: 3.5g, Sugar: 8.9g**

Ingredients

- ½ cup seedless frozen watermelon cubes
- 3 tbsp. unsweetened condensed milk
- 1½ tbsp. fresh lime juice
- Pinch of salt

Instructions

1. Blend frozen watermelon, condensed milk, fresh lime juice, and salt in a food blender until smooth, 3 minutes.
2. Transfer the sorbet mixture to the glass container/serving glass. Serve immediately or freeze until firm.

Preparing time: 5 minutes, Total time: 8 minutes, Servings: 1

TOFU STRAWBERRY SMOOTHIE

**Nutritional Info: Calories: 304cal, Total fat: 19g, Saturated fat: 0g
Protein: 18.8g, Carbs: 14.6g, Sodium: 80mg, Fiber: 4.7g, Sugar: 12g**

Ingredients

- 6 oz. tofu
- ½ cup strawberries (chopped)
- ½ cup almond milk, unsweetened
- 1 tbsp. almond butter
- ½ tsp. lemon juice
- ½ tsp. vanilla extract
- ¼ cup ice cubes
- ¼ tsp. agave nectar

Instructions

1. In the high-power blender, add all ingredients to it. Blend them well until all the elements turn into smooth form.
2. Transfer it to the serving jar/glass. Serve and enjoy.

Preparing time: 10 minutes, Total time: 10 minutes, Servings: 1

Diabetes Cookbook

FRESH FRUIT SALAD

Nutritional Info: Calories: 153cal, Total fat: 1.7g, Saturated fat: 0.1g Protein: 2.5g, Carbs: 32g, Sodium: 6mg, Fiber: 6g, Sugar: 25g

Ingredients

- ¼ cup fresh diced pineapple
- ¼ cup sliced strawberries
- ¼ cup blackberries
- ¼ cup blueberry
- ¼ cup grapes
- 1 small ripe kiwi, peeled and sliced

Instructions

1. Add pineapple, grapes, strawberries, blackberries, blueberries, and kiwi to a serving bowl.
2. Toss them well until mixed well. Serve and enjoy.

Preparing time 10 minutes, Total time 10 minutes, Servings: 1

SAUCES, DIPS AND DRESSINGS

CHEESE SAUCE

Nutritional Info: Calories: 169cal, Total fat: 14g, Saturated fat: 7g
Protein: 9g, Carbs: 1.7g, Sodium: 264mg, Fiber: 0g, Sugar: 0g

Ingredients

- 1 tbsp. low-fat whipping cream
- 1 tbsp. low-fat cream cheese
- ½ tbsp. olive oil
- Pinch of salt
- Pinch of black pepper
- 1/8 tsp. yellow mustard
- 2 tbsp. low-fat grated cheese (cheddar)

Instructions

1. Add cream cheese, olive oil, and low-fat whipping cream to a saucepan over medium heat until melted and incorporated. Add salt and pepper with mustard; stir to combine.
2. Turn off the heat. Add cheese slowly. Continue stirring until the cheese has melted entirely. Serve the cheese sauce on steamed vegetables.

Preparing time 5 minutes, Total time 10 minutes, Servings: 1

TOMATO SAUCE

Nutritional Info: Calories: 75cal, Total fat: 5.3g, Saturated fat: 1g
Protein: 1.4g, Carbs: 6g, Sodium: 112mg, Fiber: 1.6g, Sugar: 3.7g

Ingredients

- 1 tsp. extra virgin olive oil
- ½ tsp. minced garlic
- 6 tbsp. canned diced tomatoes
- Pinch of dried oregano
- ¼ tsp. white vinegar
- Pinch of salt

Instructions

1. In a saucepan, add oil over medium-high heat, and sauté the garlic in the olive oil. Sauté garlic until fragrant.
2. Decrease the stove heat and add salt, vinegar, oregano, and tomatoes to the pan. Simmer for 36-40 minutes to reduce and thicken the sauce.

Preparing time 5 minutes, Total time 45 minutes, Servings: 1

Diabetes Cookbook

TARTAR SAUCE

**Nutritional Info: Calories: 8cal, Total fat: 0g, Saturated fat: 0g
Protein: 0g, Carbs: 1.8g, Sodium: 30mg, Fiber: 0g, Sugar: 2g**

Ingredients

Sauce:
- 1 tbsp. salad dressing
- ½ tbsp. sugar-free sweet relish
- ½ tbsp. chopped fresh parsley
- Pinch of onion powder
- Pinch of black pepper

Salad Dressing:
- 1 small egg white
- 1 tsp. white wine vinegar
- Pinch of salt
- ¼ tsp. lemon juice
- Pinch of dry mustard
- ¼ tsp. paprika
- 1 tbsp. avocado oil

Instructions

1. Take all dressing elements (except oil) to bowl and beat until slightly foamy. Now slowly pour oil and beat well.
2. Take all tartar sauce elements to a small bowl. Serve with your favorite meal or save in the refrigerator until use.

Preparing time: 5 minutes, Total time: 20 minutes, Servings: 1

ALFREDO SAUCE

**Nutritional Info: Calories: 124cal, Total fat: 9g, Saturated fat: 2g
Protein: 2.6g, Carbs: 2g, Sodium: 84mg, Fiber: 0g, Sugar: 3g**

Ingredients

- 1½ tsp. olive oil
- ½ tsp. minced garlic
- ¾ tsp. low-fat cream cheese
- 1½ tbsp. shredded cottage cheese
- 2 tbsp. low-fat whipping cream
- Dash ground black pepper

Instructions

1. Add oil to the medium saucepan and put it over medium heat. Add garlic and sauté until fragrant.
2. Then place in leftover ingredients and simmer for about 10 mins or until the sauce has thickened.

Preparing time: 5 minutes, Total time: 10 minutes, Servings: 1

Diabetes Cookbook

ARTICHOKE AND SPINACH DIP

Nutritional Info: Calories: 65cal, Total fat: 2.3g, Saturated fat: 1g
Protein: 7g, Carbs: 4g, Sodium: 295mg, Fiber: 1g, Sugar: 1g

Ingredients

- 20g cooked crabmeat, shredded, discard any shell
- 30g chopped spinach
- 25g low-fat cream cheese
- 15g marinated artichoke hearts, drained and chopped
- 1/8 tsp. hot pepper sauce

Instructions

1. Add low-fat cream cheese, crabmeat, spinach, artichokes, and hot pepper sauce to a slow cooker.
2. Cover the slow cooker and cook on high for 40 minutes or until heated through, stirring after 15 minutes. Serve with toast or other meal.

Preparing time 5 minutes, Total time 45 minutes, Servings 1

DILL DIP

Nutritional Info: Calories: 26cal, Total fat: 2g, Saturated fat: 0.5g
Protein: 1.2g, Carbs: 1g, Sodium: 215mg, Fiber: 0g, Sugar: 0g

Ingredients

- 1 tbsp. fat-free sour cream
- 1 tbsp. low-fat mayonnaise
- 1/8 tsp. parsley flakes
- 1/8 tsp. onion powder
- 1/8 tsp. dill weed
- 1/8 tsp. garlic powder
- Salt to taste
- 1 drop hot sauce

Instructions

1. Add cream with mayonnaise to the mixing bowl and beat them well. Add the leftover and mix well.
2. Chill before serving to blend flavors. Serve with crunchy vegetables.

Preparing time 5 minutes, Total time 45 minutes, Servings 1

YOGURT DIP

Nutritional Info: Calories: 96cal, **Total fat:** 4g, **Saturated fat:** 0.5g
Protein: 5g, **Carbs:** 2g, **Sodium:** 260mg, **Fiber:** 2g, **Sugar:** 6g

Ingredients

- 1 tbsp. low-fat buttermilk
- 2 tbsp. low-fat plain yogurt
- 1 tbsp. low-fat mayonnaise
- 1 tsp. fresh parsley (minced)
- ¼ tsp. dried dill
- 1/8 tsp. ground garlic
- 1/8 tsp. onion powder
- Salt and black pepper to taste

Instructions

1. Add buttermilk, low-fat yogurt, mayonnaise, parsley, dill, ground garlic, onion powder, salt, and pepper to the mixing bowl.
2. Mix well until combined. If not serving immediately, store in a chilled place.

Preparing time 5 minutes, Total time 10 minutes, Servings 1

BLACK BEAN DIP

Nutritional Info: Calories: 45cal, **Total fat:** 6g, **Saturated fat:** 0g
Protein: 3g, **Carbs:** 8g, **Sodium:** 109mg, **Fiber:** 2g, **Sugar:** 2g

Ingredients

- 1½ oz. low-sodium black beans
- ½ tsp. minced garlic
- ½ tbsp. chopped green onions
- ½ tbsp. chopped parsley
- ½ tbsp. roasted red pepper
- ½ tsp. olive oil
- 1/8 tsp. chili powder
- ½ tsp. lime juice
- ¼ tsp. hot pepper sauce

Instructions

1. Place all black bean dip ingredients in the food blender, and blend until smooth. Serve as a snack or serve with vegetables, if desired.

Preparing time 5 minutes, Total time 10 minutes, Servings 1

Diabetes Cookbook

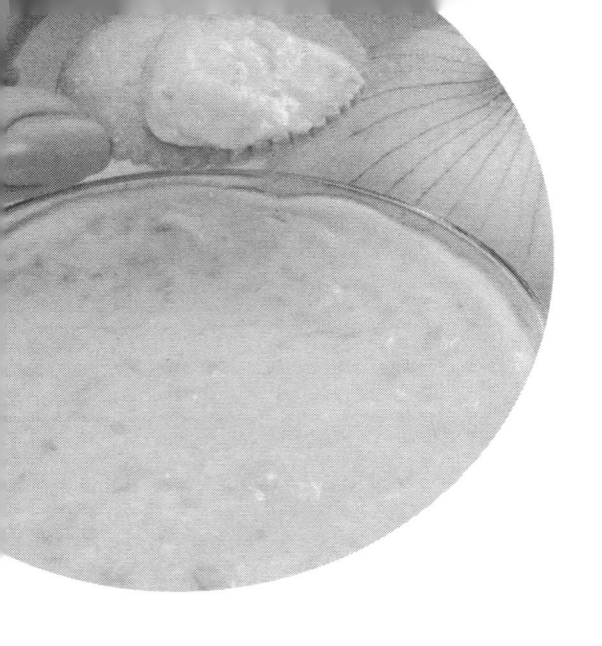

ONION DIP

Nutritional Info: Calories: 83cal, Total fat: 6g, Saturated fat: 2g
Protein: 4g, Carbs: 2.6g, Sodium: 150mg, Fiber: 2g, Sugar: 2g

Ingredients

- 15g chopped onion
- 1 tsp. extra virgin olive oil
- 2½ tbsp. low-fat cream cheese
- 20g low-fat plain yoghurt
- Salt to taste

Instructions

1. Add oil to the pan, put it over medium heat, and cook until translucent.
2. Transfer translucent onion to the blending bowl with leftover ingredients, and blend until smooth. Serve with a side dish or with snacks.

Preparing time 5 minutes, Total time 10 minutes, Servings: 1

GINGER CARROT DRESSING

Nutritional Info: Calories: 96cal, Total fat: 8g, Saturated fat: 1g
Protein: 1g, Carbs: 5g, Sodium: 35mg, Fiber: 1.4g, Sugar: 2.6g

Ingredients

- ½ tbsp. extra-virgin olive oil
- ½ tbsp. rice vinegar
- 1 small carrot, peeled and chopped
- ½ tsp. peeled and chopped fresh ginger
- ½ tsp. lime juice
- ¼ tsp. toasted sesame oil
- Sat to taste

Instructions

1. In the food blender, add all the dressing ingredients. Blend until completely smooth.
2. Add salt if needed. Spread over your favorite salad. Serve and enjoy.

Preparing time 5 minutes, Total time 5 minutes, Servings: 1

Diabetes Cookbook

CITRUS SALAD DRESSING

Nutritional Info: Calories: 76cal, **Total fat:** 6g, **Saturated fat:** 1g **Protein:** 1g, **Carbs:** 2.3g, **Sodium:** 71mg, **Fiber:** 0.2g, **Sugar:** 1.4g

Ingredients

- ½ tsp. chopped shallot
- 1 tsp. extra-virgin olive oil
- ¼ tbsp. white balsamic vinegar
- ½ tsp. freshly squeezed orange juice
- Pinch of finely grated lemon zest
- Salt and pepper to taste

Instructions

1. Add minced shallots, oil, vinegar, salt, black pepper, fresh-squeezed orange juice, and lemon zest to the small jar with a tight lid. Shake well until well mixed.

Preparing time 2 minutes, Total time 5 minutes, Servings 1

RANCH SALAD DRESSING

Nutritional Info: Calories: 43cal, **Total fat:** 3g, **Saturated fat:** 0.7g **Protein:** 2g, **Carbs:** 1.6g, **Sodium:** 243mg, **Fiber:** 0.3g, **Sugar:** 1.5g

Ingredients

- 1 tbsp. low-fat mayonnaise
- 1 tbsp. low-fat sour cream
- ¾ tsp. freshly chopped parsley
- ¼ tsp. fresh dill
- ¼ tsp. fresh chives
- ½ tsp. minced garlic
- Pinch of onion powder
- Salt and black pepper to taste
- 1½ tbsp. cow milk
- 1 tsp. lemon juice (optional)

Instructions

1. Add all the dressing elements to the small bowl. Whisk well until the ranch is smooth, and creamy, and ensure there are no lumps.
2. Add salt, pepper, and fresh lemon juice as per your like. Serve and enjoy.

Preparing time 2 minutes, Total time 5 minutes, Servings 1

Diabetes Cookbook

AVOCADO CAESAR DRESSING

Nutritional Info: Calories: 34cal, Total fat: 2g, Saturated fat: 2g
Protein: 2g, Carbs: 1.7g, Sodium: 144mg, Fiber: 0.5g, Sugar: 1g

Ingredients

- 1 tbsp. mashed avocado
- ¼ tsp. minced garlic
- ¼ tsp. Worchester sauce
- Pinch of Dijon mustard
- 2 tsp. grated parmesan cheese
- Salt and black pepper to taste
- ¼ tbsp. lemon juice
- 2 tsp. water

Instructions

1. Add all ingredients for the avocado Caesar dressing to the high-power food blender. Blend until smooth.
2. Serve right away or keep in a chilled place for next use.

Preparing time 2 minutes, Total time 5 minutes, Servings 1

BLUE CHEESE DRESSING

Nutritional Info: Calories: 30cal, Total fat: 2g, Saturated fat: 1g
Protein: 2g, Carbs: 1.4g, Sodium: 191mg, Fiber: 0g, Sugar: 0.5g

Ingredients

- 10g low-fat blue cheese
- 1 tbsp. buttermilk
- 1 tbsp. low-fat sour cream
- 1 tbsp. low-fat mayonnaise
- ¼ tsp. lemon juice
- 1/8 tsp. garlic powder
- Salt and ground black pepper to taste

Instructions

1. In a bowl, beat blue cheese with buttermilk until desired consistency is reached.
2. Then add sour cream, low-fat mayonnaise, fresh lemon juice, garlic powder, salt, and pepper.
3. Stir well until well mixed. Serve over salad and enjoy.

Preparing time 2 minutes, Total time 5 minutes, Servings 1

Diabetes Cookbook

BARBECUE SAUCE

Nutritional Info: Calories: 8cal, Total fat: 0g, Saturated fat: 0g
Protein: 0g, Carbs: 1.8g, Sodium: 30mg, Fiber: 0g, Sugar: 2g

Ingredients

- 1 tsp. tomato paste
- 1 tbsp. sugar free ketchup
- ¼ tsp. cider vinegar
- 1/8 tsp. onion powder
- ¼ tsp. Worcestershire sauce
- Pinch of salt
- 1/8 tsp. garlic powder

Instructions

1. In a saucepan, add all elements, and put it over medium heat. Bring to a boil, decrease the stove heat and simmer for about five minutes.
2. Remove from heat; then wait for 5 to 10 minutes before using. Serve with grilled fish, frankfurters, chicken, beef, or pork.

Preparing time 5 minutes, Total time 20 minutes, Servings: 1

Diabetes Cookbook

FOOD WITH GLYCEMIC INDEX

FOOD	SERVING SIZE	GI
Apples	120g	40
All-Bran	30 g	60
Apple juice	250g	39
Apricots, canned with light syrup	120g	64
Apricots, dried	60g	32
Bagel, white	70 g	69
Bananas	120g	47
Barley	150g	22
Barley flour bread, 50% wheat flour, 50% course barley flour	30g	74
Basmati rice	150g	52
Black bean soup	250g	68
Black beans	150g	30
Blueberry muffin	60g	50
Bran Buds cereal	30g	58
Bran cereal	30g	43
Bran Chex cereal	30g	58
Bran muffin	57g	60
Bread stuffing	30g	74
Broad beans	80g	79
Brown rice, steamed	50g	50
Bulgur wheat, whole, cooked	150g	46
Butter beans	150g	36
Cake, angel food	50g	67
Cake, pound	50g	38
Cantaloupe	120g	65
Carrot juice	250g	43
Carrots, raw	80g	35
Cashews	50g	25
Cheerios	30g	74
Chickpeas	150g	36
Corn chips	50g	42
Corn Flakes	30g	79
Corn syrup, dark	30g	90
Corn, sweet	80g	55

Diabetes Cookbook

FOOD	SERVING SIZE	GI
Couscous	150g	65
Croissant	57g	67
Dates	60g	62
Doughnuts, cake	47g	76
French baguette	30g	95
French bread, fermented with leaven	30g	80
French fries	150g	75
Fruit cocktail	120g	55
Gatorade	250g	78
Glucose	10g	96
Gluten-free bread, multigrain	30g	79
Gnocchi	180g	
Golden Grahams cereal	30g	71
Graham crackers	25g	74
Grape Nuts cereal	30g	75
Grapefruit	120g	25
Grapes	120g	43
Hamburger bun	30g	61
Honey, pure	25g	58
Hummus	30g	6
Ice cream, full-fat, French vanilla	50g	38
Ice cream, low-fat, vanilla, "light"	50g	46
Instant noodles	180g	52
Instant oatmeal	25 g	50
Jelly beans	30g	80
Kaiser roll	30g	73
Kidney beans	150g	29
Kidney beans, canned	150g	52
Kiwifruit	120g	58
Lentils, canned	150g	42
Life cereal	30g	66
Life Savers, peppermint	30g	70
Lima beans, baby, frozen	150g	32
Linguine, fresh, boiled	180g	61
Macaroni and cheese, boxed	180g	64

Diabetes Cookbook

FOOD	SERVING SIZE	GI
Maltose	50g	105
Mangoes	120g	51
Mixed grain bread	30g	52
Muesli	30g	86
Muesli bars, with dried apricot	30g	61
Nutri-Grain bar	30g	66
Oat bran bread	30g	44
Oat kernel bread	30g	65
Oatmeal cookies	25g	54
Oranges, raw	120g	48
Pancakes, homemade	80g	66
Parsnips, peeled boiled	80g	52
Pastry	57g	59
Peaches, canned in light syrup	120g	52
Peaches, fresh	120g	56
Pineapple	120g	51
Pita bread, white	30g	57
Pizza, cheese	100g	80
Plums	120g	53
Potato, instant, mashed,	150g	88
Potato, mashed	150g	83
Potato, microwaved	150g	93
Potato, white, boiled	150g	54
Pretzels	30g	83
Pumpernickel bread	30g	56
Pumpkin	80g	66
Raisins	60g	64
Rice cakes, white	25g	82
Rice Chex	30g	89
Rice Krispies	30g	82
Rice, instant, cooked 6 min.	150g	87
Rutabaga	15 g	72
Rye crisp-bread	25g	63
Rye flour bread, 50% rye flour, 50% wheat flour	30g	50
Rye kernel bread	30 g	41

FOOD	SERVING SIZE	GI
Shredded Wheat cereal	30g	67
Skim milk	250g	32
Snickers	60g	43
Soy milk	250g	43
Special K cereal	30g	69
Split pea soup	250g	60
Split peas, yellow, boiled	150g	25
Sponge cake	63g	46
Stoned Wheat Thins	25g	67
Strawberries	120g	40
Strawberry jam	30g	51
Sugar, table	25g	65
Sushi	100g	55
Sweet potato, boiled,	150g	61
Taco shells	20g	68
Tapioca, boiled with milk	250g	81
Tofu, frozen dessert, non-dairy	50g	115
Tomato soup	250 g	38
Total cereal	250g	76
Vanilla wafers	25g	77
Waffles	35g	76
Water crackers, whole grain, sesame seeds	25g	53
Watermelon	120g	80
White bread	30g	70
White rice, boiled	150g	47
Wild rice	150g	57

MEASUREMENT CONVERSION CHART

Dry Measurements

Measurement	Equivalent
1 pound	16 ounces
1 cup	16 tablespoons
3/4 cup	12 tablespoons
2/3 cup	10 tablespoons plus 2 teaspoons
1/2 cup	8 tablespoons
3/8 cup	6 tablespoons
1/3 cup	5 tablespoons plus 1 teaspoon
1/4 cup	4 tablespoons
1/6 cup	2 tablespoons plus 2 teaspoons
1/8 cup	2 tablespoons
1/16 cup	1 tablespoon
1 tablespoon	3 teaspoons
1/8 teaspoon	Pinch
1/16 teaspoon	Dash
1/2 cup butter	1 stick of butter

Liquid Measurements

Measurement	Equivalent
4 quarts	1 gallon
2 quarts	1/2 gallon
1 quart	1/4 gallon
2 pints	1 quart
4 cups	1 quart
2 cups	1/2 quart
2 cups	1 pint
1 cup	1/2 pint
1 cup	1/4 quart
1 cup	8 fluid ounces
3/4 cup	6 fluid ounces
2/3 cup	5.3 fluid ounces
1/2 cup	4 fluid ounces
1/3 cup	2.7 fluid ounces
1/4 cup	2 fluid ounces
1 tablespoon	0.5 fluid ounces

U.S. to Metric Conversions

Measurement	Metric Conversion
Weight Measurements	
1 pound	454 grams
8 ounces	227 grams
4 ounces	113 grams
1 ounce	28 grams
Volume Measurements	
4 quarts	3.8 liters
4 cups (1 quart)	0.95 liters
2 cups	473 milliliters
1 cup	237 milliliters
3/4 cup	177 milliliters
2/3 cup	158 milliliters
1/2 cup	118 milliliters
1/3 cup	79 milliliters
1/4 cup	59 milliliters
1/5 cup	47 milliliters
1 tablespoon	15 milliliters
1 teaspoon	5 milliliters
1/2 teaspoon	2.5 milliliters
1/5 teaspoon	1 milliliter
Fluid Measurements	
34 fluid ounces	1 liter
8 fluid ounces	237 milliliters
3.4 fluid ounces	100 milliliters
1 fluid ounce	30 milliliters

Oven Temperatures

120 C	250 F
160 C	320 F
180 C	350 F
205 C	400 F
220 C	425 F

Diabetes Cookbook

Conclusion

Having all the discussions about diabetes, now we are well aware of the disease. The only thing to keep in mind is that the lifestyle matters a lot in diabetic patients. If you are diabetic or pre-diabetic, then you must have to follow a planned and balanced diet. In this cookbook, you can get the best diet plans that are specifically designed for diabetic patients. This cookbook includes the best low-carbohydrate recipes that you can follow without fearing having increased glycaemic content. Also, some remedies can be helpful for diabetic patients.

Thank you for making it this far. I have dedicated much time to this work, and I kindly ask you, if you haven't done it yet, to help me in the disclosure of it. It would mean a lot to me if you would leave a positive review on Amazon.

Thank you!

★★★★★

Printed in Great Britain
by Amazon